T0353926

THE
VEGAN
AIR FRYER

THE

VEGAN
AIR FRYER

QUICK & EASY, HEALTHY MEALS

NIKI WEBSTER @RebelRecipes

Contents

Introduction

I am beyond excited to welcome you to *The Vegan Air Fryer*. Get ready to unleash the plant-power of your air fryer and embark on a delicious adventure with over 70 recipes that will blow your taste buds away!

My mission has always been to inspire mindful eating, making wholesome recipes that not only nourish but also celebrate the vibrancy and deliciousness of plants. You might have picked up this book because you would like to eat less meat and dairy – for your health or for environmental reasons. Perhaps you have been meat-free for a lifetime and are looking for the ease and energy-saving (yours and your home's!) that an air fryer offers. I wanted to deliver on as many different needs as possible with this book – healthy recipes, packed with nutritious ingredients; variety to suit different moods, occasions and the weather; budget-friendly cooking, and recipes that make the most of hero ingredients that are a bit more of an investment, like tahini and gochujang, but really transform a dish. I hope that whatever your tastes, you'll always find a go-to recipe in these pages to satisfy all |your cravings.

The book is divided into the main meal moments of the day and each one offers recipes that take no more than 30 minutes to rustle up. I know that sometimes we don't have 30 minutes to spare, so most of these recipes can be prepped and cooked in well under 30 minutes, and there is a chapter dedicated to meals made in 10 or 15 minutes too. Good food should be simple to make.

I've also really thought about flavour and wanted to offer a whole world of inspiration – it's the secret to amazing plant-based cooking. The right spice or seasoning will make your food sing and give you the umami hit or salty, creamy comfort that is usually associated with meat and dairy, but doesn't have to be.

From my masala cheesy crumpets to sticky mushroom burgers and spicy tofu noodles, I hope you'll have fun with these flavour-bomb meals!

I wrote this book with family cooking in mind too – those weeknight meals when inspiration is seriously needed and there is no time! That's why you'll find 'familiar' things that have an extra veg boost, like peas & greens mac 'n' cheese, and favourites, such as cheat's pizza with pesto & mushrooms (ready in just 15 minutes!).

I'm rather excited about the baking section too, as although breads and cakes are a little more challenging to cook in an air fryer, actually they turn out incredibly well! Baking in a smaller metal cake tin inside the air fryer means you can whip up a treat much faster than waiting for the oven to warm to temperature and do its thing.

Together, we're about to embark on a journey of complete deliciousness!

Love, **Niki x**

About air fryers

How do air fryers work?

These kitchen darlings have certainly transformed my cooking game, and if you haven't tried air frying yet, you're in for a treat. They're the perfect match for health-conscious foodies because they require less oil to get the same crispiness you would get in a frying pan, roasting in the oven or using a deep-fat fryer, but they don't sacrifice on flavour. Air fryers work their magic by circulating hot air to achieve that crispy perfection we all crave. From chimichurri-loaded sweet potato fries to crispy bhajis in a coconut curry and herby roast tomatoes on toast, air fryers can do it all.

And they save time! Air fryers do cook faster than conventional ovens. Vegetables get crispy and tender in a fraction of the time it would take in the oven, and you can whip up fast-cooked main meals, like mushroom souvlaki wraps and sticky sesame tacos & slaw, to save you precious minutes. For small amounts of baked goods, an air fryer can save you time since it heats up quickly and requires less time to bake than a standard oven. They're amazing for baking sweet treats (try my giant peanut butter cookie or giant cherry jam pancake), and you can have a simple soda bread or easy flatbreads on the table in no time!

These appliances are incredibly versatile and will soon become your kitchen's new best friend.

Air frying terms

BASKET
The wire drawer. This is where the magic happens! Pop your food in there and the hot air circulates around it, giving you that perfect, crispy exterior. And don't forget to preheat the air fryer with the basket inside for top-notch results.

BAKING TRAY/TINS
Metal tray – This is typically a small, flat metal tray/tin. Find one to fit your air fryer. Great for baking, roasting and toasting, you can use an air fryer-specific one or a standard metal tray/tin that fits inside.

Silicone tray – This is flexible and you can find many to fit your air fryer exactly. I use them for roasting veg when I want to keep the juices. Silicone liners are also a game-changer for clean-up.

Cake tin – I used an air fryer high-sided metal tin to bake the bread in for this book and a standard loaf tin for the coconut/banana bread.

AIR FRYER BASE/BOTTOM
By this, I mean the bottom of the air fryer. You can put ingredients directly into the base. I use this technique for cooking pasta recipes and stews.

BAKING PAPER AND OIL SPRAYS
Baking paper – Used for cooking cookies (with or without small holes in the bottom).

Oil misters or sprays – These are kitchen magicians! With a little spritz here and there, you get that crispy texture we adore without drowning your food in oil.

Tips and tricks

I want to share some tips and tricks that will help you make the most of your air fryer experience. As with any kitchen tool, each air fryer has its little quirks. They come in different shapes and sizes, and cooking times might vary a bit.

To achieve air fryer excellence, keep these pointers in mind:

- Depending on your air fryer, you might need to adjust the cooking time and temperature slightly.
- Preheating your air fryer is a crucial step to ensure accurate cooking at your desired temperature. Trust me, it's worth it!
- When it comes to roasting veggies, cut them evenly to ensure every bite is as crispy and satisfying as the last.
- Don't overcrowd the air fryer basket. Give your food some space to breathe and it'll reward you with irresistible crispiness.
- Midway through cooking, don't forget to give your basket a gentle shake to ensure everything gets cooked to perfection on all sides.
- And speaking of baking, I found that using a metal baking tin yields the best results. Silicone trays can be a bit tricky when it comes to achieving an evenly cooked base and centre of the cake. So, for a perfectly baked treat, I highly recommend opting for a metal baking tin instead.

There are lots of different sizes of air fryers, but for most recipes in this cookbook, I found a small Ninja worked perfectly. However, for some of the mains, I suggest a dual air fryer, if you have one, because it gives more capacity and you can cook multiple components of a dish at the same time. However, it isn't essential and you can cook in batches, if necessary.

Healthy cooking:
Plant-based vs vegan

Before we dive headfirst into the recipes, let's take a moment to understand the distinction between veganism and a plant-based diet. Veganism is not just about what's on our plates, it's a way of living that seeks to exclude, as far as possible and practicable, all forms of exploitation and cruelty to animals – for food, clothing or any other purpose.

On the other hand, a plant-based diet centres around wholesome foods like vegetables, fruits, pulses, grains, nuts and seeds, with a focus on nourishing our bodies and celebrating the beauty of plants.

This cookbook is a celebration of healthy choices, both for you and the planet. I'm all about embracing the wonders of whole foods, fresh and vibrant vegetables, and the beauty of plant-based eating to give you a powerhouse of nutrients to fuel your body and mind.

Whether you're a seasoned plant-based pro or someone just starting to explore the world of vibrant veggies, this cookbook offers simple inspiration. And choosing plant-based meals is a win-win for both you and the planet. By embracing more plant-powered goodness and reducing meat consumption, you're having a positive impact on the environment. Plant-based diets are recognised for their sustainability, contributing to lower greenhouse gas emissions. So, with each plant-based meal you cook from this book, you're contributing to a brighter, greener future for all of us.

The focus of this book is on fresh whole foods. However, where I think it will make the recipe even more delicious, I have suggested adding some shop-bought, more processed ingredients like vegan cheese and dairy. They add extra gooeyness or creaminess to a dish but are not essential. I have listed some of my tried-and-tested products in the next section, but you may have your own favourites.

Cook's notes

These are air fryer recipes and the mission of this book is to help you get the most out of your air fryer, but there are some ingredients that taste infinitely better not cooked in the air fryer and I don't want to compromise on flavour. So, you'll see that onions, garlic, spices and sauces are cooked in a frying pan at the same time as the other elements of the dish are cooking in the air fryer. I'm sorry if this annoys anyone, but I promise it is worth it!

As the book is called *The Vegan Air Fryer*, I have not said 'vegan cheese', 'plant-based butter' etc throughout the ingredients lists in the recipes. However, every recipe here has been tested using vegan alternatives.

Please check product labels carefully to make sure they are vegan. For example, it might surprise you that things like gnocchi and Worcestershire sauce (used in this book) aren't always vegan, but you can buy vegan versions relatively easily these days.

I thought it might be useful to tell you which brands I used to cook the recipes in this book, particularly if you are new to plant-based eating and are not sure where to start:

- Naturli' Vegan Block is fantastic as a buttery spread.
- Oatly Barista milk works well to create creamy, dreamy sauces.
- For melty Cheddar cheese-style substitutes, I rate Applewood, Ilchester and Cathedral City. These brands make scrumptious and melty vegan cheeses.
- More expensive but particularly delicious are Julienne Bruno and La Fauxmagerie for cheeses too.
- Doves Farm flours deliver on quality and variety and are a good brand if you would like to use an organic flour.
- Belazu's vegan pastes and sauces add immediate flavour to your creations.

easy breakfasts

MORNING

Chewy banana breakfast cookie

Who doesn't love a breakfast cookie? And these are fast enough to be whipped up before school or work. You can mix in any additions you fancy: choc chips, dried fruit, nuts and seeds.

MAKES 1 LARGE COOKIE
READY IN 15 MINUTES

DRY INGREDIENTS
**75g (¾ cup) oats of choice/
 rolled oats**
1 tsp baking powder
½ tsp ground cinnamon
3 tbsp ground almonds
**2 tbsp sunflower seeds,
 plus extra for topping**

WET INGREDIENTS
**2 ripe bananas, peeled
 and mashed**
2 tbsp peanut butter
1 tbsp milk
1 tbsp maple syrup

Preheat your air fryer to 180°C (350°F) for 2 minutes.

Line an 18cm baking tin with baking paper.

Mix the dry ingredients in a bowl.

In a separate bowl, mix the wet ingredients, then add to the dry mix. Mix everything together well to form a sticky mixture.

Put the mixture in the baking tin and form into a large cookie shape.

Top with sunflower seeds and air fry for 7–9 minutes, depending on how gooey you'd like the middle to be.

Fruity warm oat pot

The perfect warming breakfast. A cross between baked oats and porridge as the centre is a little gooey. You add any fruit you fancy: blueberries, blackberries and banana are all delicious!

SERVES 1–2
READY IN 15 MINUTES

Oil spray
60g (generous ½ cup) oats of choice/rolled oats
250ml (½ cup) oat or other milk
2 tbsp brown/demerara sugar
½ tsp ground cinnamon
100g (scant 1 cup) raspberries

Preheat the air fryer to 180°C (350°F) for 2 minutes.

Spray or grease a 14–16cm (5½–6¼ inch) ovenproof dish or pan.

Add the oats, milk, sugar, cinnamon and raspberries. Stir to combine.

Air fry for 12 minutes, stirring once.

Banana & blueberry baked oats

Baked banana and blueberry oats with a little peanut butter for some plant-based protein and just because it's a dream combination with banana. This makes a delicious breakfast for one with a good appetite or for two with some plain yogurt and fruit.

SERVES 1
READY IN 10 MINUTES

75g (¾ cup) oats of choice/ rolled oats

1 very ripe medium banana, peeled

1 tbsp nut butter of choice

½ tsp vanilla extract

¼ tsp baking powder

1 tbsp sweetener (I used maple syrup)

2 tbsp milk

75g (½ cup) blueberries

Preheat your air fryer to 150°C (300°F) for 2 minutes.

Put all the ingredients (apart from the blueberries) into a food processor and blitz until you get a nice smooth texture.

Spoon into a ramekin and stir in the blueberries.

Air fry for 9 minutes, until cooked but still a little gooey inside.

Coconut bread
with gooey banana

Easy to make, with a tropical coconut and banana taste, I love this topped with jam, Greek-style yogurt and gooey roast banana. You can also toast it if you prefer. It's important not to use a silicone tin for this to ensure the base is cooked properly.

SERVES 8–10
READY IN 35 MINUTES

1 large ripe banana, peeled
100g (scant ½ cup) caster sugar
100g (1 cup) ground almonds (almond meal)
1 tsp apple cider vinegar
200ml (generous ¾ cup) milk
50g (generous ½ cup) desiccated coconut
120g (generous ¾ cup) plain flour
1 tsp baking powder
1 tsp vanilla extract

TO SERVE
1 banana
Splash of maple syrup
Jam of choice
Greek-style yogurt

Preheat the air fryer to 165°C (330°F) for 2 minutes.

Grease or line a loaf tin with baking paper.

Add all the ingredients to a food processor and blitz until smooth. Transfer the mix to the loaf tin and smooth out the top.

Air fry for 25–30 minutes, or until the bread is cooked in the centre. Test the centre is cooked by inserting a skewer – it should come out clean. Allow the bread to cool before slicing.

At the same time, slice the skin of the remaining banana along the top. Open it a little and then slice the banana (in the skin) into chunks. Drizzle with a splash of maple syrup.

Add to the air fryer along with the cake. Air fry for about 15–20 minutes, removing when bubbling.

Top the bread slices with jam and yogurt and serve with the roast banana.

Cheesy French toast
with avocado salsa

I love how fluffy these cheesy slices of French toast become when cooked in an air fryer. The addition of cheese and Worcestershire sauce makes them taste like Welsh rarebit – so good! Top with avocado salsa for a weekend brunch or serve with baked beans when in need of a filling lunch.

SERVES 4
READY IN 25 MINUTES

100ml (scant ½ cup) milk
75g (½ cup) self-raising flour
1 tsp Dijon mustard
1 tbsp Worcestershire sauce
50g (½ cup) grated smoked cheese
4 slices of fresh bread
Oil spray

FOR THE SALSA
200g (1⅓ cups) cherry tomatoes, sliced into chunks
1 ripe avocado, sliced into small chunks
1 tbsp extra virgin olive oil
10g (¼oz) fresh coriander (cilantro), finely chopped
Juice of ½ lime

To make the French toast, in a bowl, whisk together the milk, flour, mustard, Worcestershire sauce and cheese. Season with a pinch of sea salt.

Spoon the batter into a shallow dish, then add each slice of bread and flip to coat both sides.

Preheat the air fryer to 200°C (400°F) for 2 minutes.

Spray a baking tin with oil spray. Add the bread but don't overcrowd.

Air fry for 4–5 minutes, turning once, then cook for 2 more minutes until puffed up and golden brown. Repeat with any remaining slices.

To make the salsa, put all the ingredients in a bowl and toss to combine. Season to taste.

Top the French toast with the salsa.

Smoky potato breakfast hash

If you're after a savoury brunch dish that's packed with flavour and is super nutritious, this is a great one. Shaving the tofu means it's thin and gets very crispy, which adds great texture, as well as plant-based protein.

SERVES 4
READY IN 25 MINUTES

350g (12oz) potatoes, peeled and chopped into 1.5cm (⅝ inch) cubes
2 tbsp olive oil
1 leek, trimmed and chopped
1 red (bell) pepper, deseeded and sliced
2 flat mushrooms, sliced
1 tbsp smoked paprika
1 tsp cumin seeds
Pinch of chilli flakes
2 tomatoes, chopped
150g (5½oz) smoked firm tofu, pressed
Juice of ½ lime
1 ripe avocado, sliced
Fresh coriander (cilantro)

Preheat your air fryer to 200°C (400°F) for 2 minutes.

Put the potatoes in a baking tin with 1 tablespoon of the olive oil and some sea salt. Air fry for 10 minutes, shaking occasionally, then set aside.

In the meantime, fry the leek with the remaining olive oil in a frying pan for 6–7 minutes until soft. Now add in the red pepper and mushrooms.

Add the spices and tomatoes and cook for 2–3 minutes.

Shave the tofu into thin strips with a peeler or cut carefully with a knife. Put the tofu and a pinch of sea salt into the baking tin and air fry for 6–7 minutes, until crispy, shaking occasionally.

Add the tofu to the vegetable mix along with the potatoes and stir to combine.

To serve, top the smoky potatoes with lime juice, sliced avocado and lots of coriander.

Breakfast bagels
with sticky tofu & mushrooms

Air frying the thinly sliced tofu and mushrooms makes the texture crispy and the flavour a little 'meaty', so these extremely tasty bagels are going to impress. I love them with hummus and mayo, but sliced tomatoes or gherkins would also be fantastic.

SERVES 4
READY IN 15 MINUTES

225g (8oz) smoked firm tofu, pressed

125g (4½oz) chestnut mushrooms

4 bagels, halved

Hummus

Sour cream/mayo

Fresh herbs of choice

FOR THE DRESSING

3 tablespoons soy sauce/ tamari

2 tbsp Worcestershire sauce

2 tbsp maple syrup

1 tbsp apple cider vinegar

1 tbsp smoked paprika

1 tbsp garlic powder

2 tbsp olive oil

Preheat your air fryer to 200°C (400°F) for 2 minutes.

Shave the tofu and mushrooms into thin slices with a peeler and put in a bowl.

In a jar, mix the dressing ingredients together. Add to the bowl and mix to combine.

Transfer to a baking tin and air fry for 5 minutes. Mix and cook for a further 5 minutes, until slightly crispy.

In the meantime, toast the bagels.

To serve, top the bottom half of the bagels with hummus, then crispy tofu. Spread sour cream/mayo over the top halves and sandwich together with the herbs.

Tofu scramble roll
with dill yogurt

A high protein and very tasty breakfast or brunch idea. The scramble contains a little cheese, which makes everything gooey. Just as good on slices of chunky toast.

SERVES 4
READY IN 15 MINUTES

225g (8oz) firm tofu, pressed and crumbled

8 cherry tomatoes, chopped

2 spring onions (scallions), sliced

2 mushrooms, finely chopped

4 tbsp grated cheese (optional)

2 tbsp soy sauce/tamari

1 tsp garlic powder

4 tbsp nutritional yeast

4 ciabatta rolls, sliced

FOR THE DILL YOGURT

4 tbsp Greek-style yogurt

Big handful of fresh dill, chopped

Preheat your air fryer to 200°C (400°F) for 2 minutes.

For the tofu, put the tofu in a bowl with the tomatoes, spring onions, mushrooms, grated cheese and all the seasonings. Toss to coat.

Add the mix to a baking tin and air fry for 5 minutes. Stir and cook for a further 5 minutes.

To make the dill yogurt, mix both ingredients in a jar and season well.

To serve, toast the rolls. Top the rolls with some dill yogurt, tofu scramble and more dollops of dill yogurt.

Spiced veggie frittata

This recipe is great for brunch or lunch with a big salad. The 'eggy' part is made from a combination of silken tofu, gram flour and spices with some grated cheese stirred in. This is then added to the air-fried roast vegetables and baked.

SERVES ABOUT 6
READY IN 30 MINUTES

150g (5½oz) mushrooms, sliced

1 red or green (bell) pepper, deseeded and sliced

1 courgette (zucchini), sliced

1 tbsp olive oil

Balsamic glaze

Salad

FOR THE FRITTATA MIX

200g (7oz) silken tofu

1 tsp garam masala

1 tsp baking powder

¼ tsp ground turmeric

70g (generous ½ cup) gram flour (besan)

1 tbsp apple cider vinegar

50g (½ cup) grated cheese

Preheat the air fryer to 180°C (350°F) for 2 minutes.

Add the sliced vegetables to a baking tin, drizzle with the olive oil and sprinkle with a pinch of sea salt.

Air fry for 4–6 minutes, until soft and slightly charred. Drain if the mushrooms produce any liquid.

To make the frittata, put all the ingredients except the cheese into a food processor and blend until you have a smooth and creamy mix. Season to taste. Add the grated cheese and blitz again briefly.

Now add the frittata mix to the roast veg and stir to combine. Smooth out the top.

Air fry for approx. 10–12 minutes, until set throughout and a little brown on top.

Slice, drizzle with balsamic and serve with a salad.

Herby roast tomatoes on toast

A simple but absolutely delicious brunch dish. The cherry tomatoes are cooked in super-quick time, so this can be whipped up quickly, and beans add great plant-based protein.

SERVES 2
READY IN 15 MINUTES

250g (generous 1½ cups) cherry tomatoes
3 tbsp extra virgin olive oil, plus more for drizzling
1 tsp dried oregano
2 tbsp fresh thyme leaves, plus more to garnish
2 slices of chunky bread

FOR THE CRUSHED BUTTER BEANS
1 tin of butter beans, drained
Juice of ½ lemon
1 tbsp extra virgin olive oil
1 tbsp tahini

Preheat your air fryer to 180°C (350°F) for 2 minutes.

Place the tomatoes in a baking tin and toss with a splash of extra virgin olive oil and some sea salt. Air fry for about 7 minutes, tossing halfway through.

Transfer to a bowl and add the dried oregano, fresh thyme and 1–2 tablespoons of the extra virgin olive oil and season to taste.

In the meantime, put the butter beans into a bowl along with the lemon juice, extra virgin olive oil and tahini. With a fork, mash roughly and season well.

For the charred bread, heat a griddle pan or frying pan to medium. Add a splash of oil, then transfer the bread to the pan. Cook on each side until a little charred on both sides.

To serve, top the toast with the smashed beans and roast tomatoes and their juices. Drizzle with more oil and sprinkle some fresh thyme over the top.

Masala cheesy crumpets

An incredible cheese on toast, pizza, masala toast hybrid!
For breakfast, brunch or a snack, these are fantastic!

SERVES 2–4
READY IN 5 MINUTES

4 tbsp grated cheese

¼ red chilli, deseeded and finely sliced

½ tsp ground cumin

½ red onion, very finely chopped

3 tbsp chopped fresh coriander (cilantro)

4 crumpets

4 tbsp sun-dried tomato paste

Preheat the air fryer to 180°C (350°F) for 2 minutes.

Mix the cheese, chilli, cumin, red onion and coriander in a bowl.

Top each crumpet with 1 tablespoon of sun-dried tomato paste, then top with the cheese mix.

In a baking tin, air fry the topped crumpets for 3 minutes, until crispy and the cheese has melted.

simple
lunches
&
lighter
bites

TAKE A BREAK

Creamy roast veg soup *with chickpeas* **52**

Roasted tomato & pepper soup *with pesto bread* **55**

Curried sweet potato soup **56**

Charred sweetcorn soup **59**

Roast veg salsa *with smoky pitta chips* **60**

Root veg grain bowl *with olives & toasted hazelnuts* **62**

Cheesy pea arancini **64**

Aubergine meze on toast **66**

Spiced-rice stuffed peppers **69**

Chimichurri-loaded sweet potato fries **70**

Courgette & sweetcorn fritters *with sesame sauce* **73**

Jacket potato boats *with harissa beans* **74**

Smoky jackfruit sliders **76**

Roast pepper pesto & cheese toastie **78**

Bombay potato toasted sandwich **80**

Loaded pea falafel pockets **82**

Roast Potatoes & Courgettes *with garlicky green yogurt* **85**

Creamy roast veg soup

with chickpeas

Roasting veg in the air fryer is an amazing way to make a delicious soup in super-quick time! I've added chickpeas for protein and coconut cream for a little indulgence, but you could leave it out for a lower-fat option.

SERVES 4
READY IN 25 MINUTES

- 300g (10½oz) sweet potatoes, peeled and cut into small cubes
- 100g (3½oz) carrots, peeled and cut into small cubes
- 2 tbsp olive oil
- 2 red (bell) peppers, deseeded and chopped
- 4 cloves garlic, sliced
- 1 tsp ground cumin
- 1 tbsp smoked paprika
- 750ml (3 cups) vegetable stock
- 2 tbsp coconut cream/ plain yogurt (optional), plus more to garnish
- Pinch of pul biber chilli flakes
- Handful of tinned chickpeas (garbanzos), drained

Preheat your air fryer to 180°C (350°F) for 2 minutes.

Put the sweet potatoes, carrots, 1 tablespoon of the olive oil and some sea salt and black pepper into the basket. Air fry for 15 minutes, shaking occasionally.

Meanwhile, put the red peppers in a large pan with the remaining olive oil and sauté for 6–7 minutes on a low/medium heat. Add the garlic and fry for 1 minute. Now add the spices and fry for a further minute.

Next, add the cooked sweet potatoes, carrots and veg stock to the pan and simmer for 2 minutes, covered. Season generously with sea salt and black pepper.

Turn off the heat, then blitz using an immersion blender until smooth and creamy, adding some water if you'd like it thinner. Stir in the coconut cream/yogurt, if using.

Ladle the soup into bowls. To finish, top with a swirl of coconut cream/yogurt, a sprinkle of chilli flakes and the chickpeas.

Roasted tomato & pepper soup

with pesto bread

This vibrant soup is easy to make as all the veg is roasted in the air fryer, then blitzed to a creamy soup. And with the pesto bread dipped in – oh, my goodness!

SERVES 4
READY IN 25 MINUTES

3 red (bell) peppers, deseeded and cut into small cubes

250g (1⅔ cups) cherry tomatoes

4 tbsp extra virgin olive oil

1 onion, sliced

3 cloves garlic, sliced

1 tsp smoked paprika

1 tsp cumin seeds

2 tbsp sun-dried tomato paste

250ml (1 cup) vegetable stock

2 slices of fresh bread of choice

Pesto (see page 91) or shop bought

Preheat your air fryer to 200°C (400°F) for 2 minutes.

To make the soup, put the red peppers, tomatoes, 1 tablespoon of the extra virgin olive oil and some sea salt and black pepper in a baking tin.

Air fry for 5 minutes, shake and cook for a further 5 minutes.

In the meantime, fry your onion and garlic in a frying pan with 2 tablespoons of the olive oil for 6–7 minutes. Add the spices and fry for a further minute.

Now add the sun-dried tomato paste, stock and the roast veg and simmer for 5 minutes. Season well. Turn off the heat and then blitz until smooth with an immersion blender. Ladle into soup bowls.

To toast your bread, top the bread with pesto, then add to the basket and air fry for 3 minutes.

To serve, drizzle the soup with the remaining olive oil and some pesto and serve with the pesto toasts.

Curried sweet potato soup

A lightly spiced, golden, nourishing soup perfect for lunches and light meals. Roasting the sweet potatoes and carrots in the air fryer means you can add tons of roasted flavour in super-fast time.

SERVES 4
READY IN 25 MINUTES

400g (14oz) sweet potatoes, peeled and cut into small cubes

200g (7oz) carrots, peeled and cut into small cubes

2 tbsp olive oil

2 leeks, trimmed and sliced

4 cloves garlic, sliced

2 tsp grated (peeled) fresh ginger

1 tsp cumin seeds

½ tsp ground turmeric

1 litre (4 cups) vegetable stock

3 tbsp cream/plain yogurt, plus more to garnish

Pinch of pul biber chilli flakes

Fresh coriander (cilantro)

Preheat your air fryer to 180°C (350°F) for 2 minutes.

Put the sweet potatoes, carrots, 1 tablespoon of the olive oil and some sea salt and black pepper into the basket. Air fry for about 15 minutes, shaking occasionally.

Meanwhile, put the leek in a large pan with the remaining olive oil and sauté for 6–7 minutes on a low/medium heat. Add the garlic and ginger and fry for 1 minute. Now add the spices and fry for a further minute.

Next, add the cooked sweet potatoes, carrots and veg stock to the pan and simmer for 2 minutes, covered. Season generously with sea salt and black pepper.

Turn off the heat and then blitz using an immersion blender until smooth and creamy, adding some water if you'd like it thinner. Stir in the cream or yogurt. Ladle into soup bowls.

To finish, top with a swirl of cream or yogurt, a sprinkle of chilli flakes and some fresh coriander.

Charred sweetcorn soup

Creamy and luscious, this soup is reminiscent of a corn chowder but with a little added spice. The corn becomes sweet and lightly roasted in the air fryer, which adds amazing flavour to the soup. I love making this when sweetcorn is in season.

SERVES 4
READY IN 20 MINUTES

4 corn on the cobs
2 tbsp olive oil
1 leek, trimmed and sliced
3 cloves garlic, sliced
½ thumb of fresh ginger, peeled and minced
1 tsp chopped green chilli
1 tin of light coconut milk
350ml (scant 1½ cups) vegetable stock
Roasted salted peanuts, crushed
Fresh coriander (cilantro)
1 green chilli, deseeded and finely sliced

Carefully remove all the kernels from the corn on the cobs using a sharp knife.

Preheat the air fryer to 180°C (350°F) for 2 minutes.

Place the corn in a baking tin, drizzle with 1 tablespoon of the olive oil and sprinkle over some sea salt.

Air fry the corn for 10 minutes, until starting to turn golden brown, shaking occasionally.

In the meantime, fry the leek in a large saucepan with the remaining olive oil for 6–8 minutes. Add the garlic, ginger and chopped chilli and fry for a minute or so.

Transfer three-quarters of the corn to the pan along with the coconut milk and vegetable stock. Cook for 3–4 minutes, then blitz with an immersion blender to your desired consistency (you can keep it chunky or blend until very smooth). Season to taste.

Serve topped with crushed peanuts, coriander, the reserved corn and the green chilli slices.

Roast veg salsa
with smoky pitta chips

This salsa is perfect for snacking or for parties, served alongside more dips and bread etc. Roasting all the veg in the air fryer saves lots of time and also adds flavour. The genius smoky pitta chips make the perfect accompaniment to scoop everything up with!

SERVES 4
READY IN 25 MINUTES

4 tomatoes (approx. 300g/10½oz), halved

3 cloves garlic, peeled

1 red (bell) pepper, deseeded and quartered

2 red onions, cut into chunks

3 tbsp extra virgin olive oil

1 tsp ground cumin

½ red chilli, chopped

Juice of 1 lime

30g (1oz) fresh coriander (cilantro)/mint, plus more (chopped) to garnish

Plain yogurt

FOR THE PITTAS
3 pittas

1 tbsp extra virgin olive oil

1 tsp smoked paprika

Preheat your air fryer to 180°C (350°F) for 2 minutes.

Add the tomatoes, cloves of garlic, red pepper and onions to a baking tin. Drizzle with a splash of the extra virgin olive oil and sprinkle with sea salt.

Air fry for 6 minutes, then remove the garlic. Cook for a further 6–7 minutes.

Transfer all the cooked veg, including the garlic, to a food processor along with the juices and all the remaining ingredients, except the yogurt. Blitz to a chunky paste.

For the pittas, tear the pittas into bite-sized pieces and add to a large bowl. Drizzle with the extra virgin olive oil, smoked paprika and some sea salt and toss to coat. Spread the pitta chips in the basket.

Air fry on 180°C (350°F) for 4–5 minutes, until golden and crisp, shaking the basket occasionally.

To serve, top the salsa with yogurt and extra chopped herbs and dip in the pitta chips.

Root veg grain bowl
with olives & toasted hazelnuts

Bursting with healthy veg, grains and pulses, this is not only super nutritious, it also packs a flavour and a texture punch and will keep you fuller for longer. You can use any grain or pulse you fancy.

SERVES 2
READY IN 30 MINUTES

300g (10½oz) sweet potatoes, peeled and cut into small cubes

100g (3½oz) carrots, peeled and cut into small cubes

6 tbsp extra virgin olive oil

1 large red onion, cut into strips

Handful of spinach, chopped

250g (9oz) cooked grain of choice (I used rice)

1 tin of chickpeas (garbanzos), drained

50g (⅓ cup) roasted hazelnuts

4 dried apricots, finely chopped

70g (generous ½ cup) pitted green olives, sliced

30g (1oz) fresh mint/dill/thyme

FOR THE DRESSING
3 tbsp apple cider vinegar
Juice of 1 lemon
1 large clove garlic, grated
1 tsp maple syrup

Preheat your air fryer to 180°C (350°F) for 2 minutes.

Put the sweet potatoes, carrots, 1 tablespoon of the extra virgin olive oil and some sea salt and black pepper into the basket. Air fry for about 15 minutes, shaking occasionally.

In the meantime, fry the onion in 1 tablespoon of the extra virgin olive oil in a saucepan for 5–6 minutes until soft.

Now add in all the remaining ingredients, plus the cooked sweet potatoes and carrots when they are ready. Mix to combine and cook for a few minutes until heated through.

For the dressing, combine all the ingredients with the remaining 4 tablespoons of extra virgin olive oil in a jar and shake to combine. Season to taste.

Pour the dressing over the veg and grain mixture and mix well. Season with sea salt and black pepper to taste and divide into bowls to serve.

Cheesy pea arancini

The best way to use up leftover risotto – make crispy arancini balls! Or you can just cook up a batch of Arborio rice specially. Serve with pesto and garlic mayo – YUM! It's best to use a dual air fryer here, but if you don't have one, just cook in batches.

MAKES 18 ARANCINI
READY IN 25 MINUTES

800g (generous 4 cups) cooked risotto or Arborio rice

150g (1 cup) frozen peas, defrosted

Juice of ½ lemon

50g (½ cup) grated cheese

200g (7oz) toasted bread

Fresh basil leaves, shredded

Pesto (see page 91) or shop bought

Garlic mayo

To make the arancini, mix the cooked rice with the peas, lemon juice and cheese in a bowl. Now scoop up into golf ball-sized amounts and roll into balls. Place the balls on a plate ready for coating.

To make the crumb, break up the toast a little, add to your food processor and blitz until you get a fine crumb. Season to taste. Transfer the crumb mixture to a large plate. Roll each ball in the crumb to coat all over.

Preheat the air fryer to 170°C (340°F) for 2 minutes.

Place the crumb-coated balls in a single layer in the basket and air fry for approx. 10 minutes, until golden and crispy, turning once.

Serve the arancini with shredded basil leaves, pesto and garlic mayo.

Aubergine meze on toast

Aubergines are roasted, then tossed into a rich tomato and pepper stew. Brilliant on toast, but also amazing as a jacket potato or rice topper, or try as part of a meze platter with hummus and breads.

SERVES 4
READY IN 20 MINUTES

2 small aubergines (eggplants), sliced

4 tbsp extra virgin olive oil

1 red onion, sliced into 5mm (¼ inch) thick rounds

4 cloves garlic, sliced

4 tomatoes, chopped

2 tbsp sun-dried tomato paste

1 tsp ground turmeric

1 red (bell) pepper, deseeded and cut into small cubes

20g (¾oz) fresh mint leaves, shredded

Juice of ½ lemon

4 tbsp plain yogurt

1 clove garlic, grated

4 slices of toasted bread

Fresh coriander (cilantro)/ mint, chopped/shredded

Preheat your air fryer to 200°C (400°F) for 2 minutes.

To cook the aubergines, put the aubergine slices, 1 tablespoon of the extra virgin olive oil and some sea salt and black pepper into the basket. Air fry for 11–12 minutes, shaking occasionally.

Meanwhile, add the remaining 3 tablespoons of the extra virgin olive oil and the onion to a frying pan and cook for 6–8 minutes until soft. Add the sliced garlic and fry for 30 seconds more.

Now add the tomatoes, tomato paste and turmeric and simmer down for 5 minutes. Add the aubergine, red pepper, mint, some sea salt and black pepper and the lemon juice.

To make the garlic sauce, add the yogurt and grated garlic to a jar and mix to combine. Season well.

To serve, top the toast with the aubergine meze, garlic yogurt sauce and herbs of choice.

Spiced-rice stuffed peppers

Perfect for lunch, I love these roasted peppers served with some crunchy slaw and fresh bread. You can swap the rice for quinoa, couscous or bulgur wheat. The cheese is optional, just skip the final step if you aren't adding it.

SERVES 2–4
READY IN 20 MINUTES

2 red/orange (bell) peppers, halved and deseeded

2 tbsp extra virgin olive oil

6 spring onions (scallions), chopped

3 cloves garlic, sliced

1 tsp ground cumin

1 tsp ground coriander

1 tsp ground turmeric

½ tsp chilli flakes

2 tomatoes, roughly chopped

Splash of water

200g (generous 1 cup) cooked rice

2 tbsp coconut yogurt/cream/milk

4 tbsp grated cheese (vegan melty)

Preheat your air fryer to 180°C (350°F) for 2 minutes.

Place the red/orange peppers in the basket. Drizzle with a splash of the extra virgin olive oil and season. Air fry until the peppers are tender, about 12 minutes.

To make the rice, put the remaining extra virgin olive oil and the spring onions in a frying pan and fry for 2–3 minutes, then add the garlic and spices.

Cook for a further minute, then add the tomatoes and water. Simmer down for 2–3 minutes. Now add the cooked rice and yogurt/cream/milk. Stir to combine and heat through.

To serve, spoon the rice mix into the cooked peppers in the basket, then top with cheese.

Air fry on 200°C (400°F) for 2–3 minutes more or until the cheese has melted.

Chimichurri-loaded sweet potato fries

These fries are completely more-ish and perfect for parties and healthy snacking. The chimichurri is also amazing on most roast veg or with a fresh tomato salad.

SERVES 2
READY IN 15 MINUTES

350g (12oz) sweet potatoes, peeled and sliced into 5mm (¼ inch) thick sticks
1 tbsp olive oil
1 tsp garlic powder
1 tsp smoked paprika

FOR THE CHIMICHURRI
30g (1oz) fresh flat-leaf parsley
4 cloves garlic, peeled
1 banana shallot, peeled
1 tsp dried oregano
½ large red chilli, deseeded
5 tbsp red wine vinegar
50ml (scant ¼ cup) extra virgin olive oil

Preheat your air fryer to 190°C (375°F) for 2 minutes.

Place the sweet potatoes in a mixing bowl and toss with the olive oil, garlic powder, smoked paprika and some sea salt and black pepper.

Arrange on a baking tin without overcrowding (you might need to cook in batches). Air fry for 6 minutes, shake and then cook for another 2–3 minutes.

For the chimichurri, put all the ingredients into a food processor and blitz to a chunky paste. Season generously.

To serve, top the sweet potato fries with the chimichurri.

Courgette & sweetcorn fritters

with sesame sauce

These addictively good fritters are absolutely brilliant for packed lunches or a healthy snack. It's important to get as much moisture as possible out of the grated courgettes so they aren't soggy.

MAKES ABOUT 12 FRITTERS
READY IN 30 MINUTES

250g (9oz) courgettes (zucchini), grated

200g (1⅓ cups) self-raising flour

1 tsp garlic powder

2 tbsp nutritional yeast (optional)

4 spring onions (scallions), sliced

3 tbsp chopped fresh dill/ mint

165g tinned sweetcorn, drained

125ml (½ cup) water

Oil spray

FOR THE DIPPING SAUCE

4 tbsp soy sauce/tamari

2 tbsp rice vinegar

4 tbsp toasted sesame oil

4 tbsp sweet chilli sauce

To make the fritters, grate and salt the courgette for about 5 minutes, then drain – this helps remove as much moisture as possible.

Put the courgettes, flour, a pinch of sea salt and black pepper, the garlic powder and nutritional yeast (if using) in a large bowl. Stir to combine. Add in the spring onions, herbs, sweetcorn and water and mix together.

Preheat your air fryer to 180°C (350°F) for 2 minutes.

To make the dipping sauce, mix the ingredients in a jar.

Spray a baking tin with a little oil. Add a heaped tablespoon of the batter to the tin and flatten a little so you get a roundish pancake. Repeat to fill the tin. Spray or brush with a little more oil.

Air fry for 5 minutes, then flip and cook for another 3 minutes, or until cooked through. Repeat with any remaining mixture.

Jacket potato boats

with harissa beans

Jacket potatoes with a perfect crispy skin, fluffy centre and homemade beans – so simple but so good! A brilliant weeknight dinner or lunch for the whole family.

SERVES 4
READY IN 35 MINUTES

2 baking potatoes, halved into boat shapes
1 tbsp extra virgin olive oil
3 tbsp plain yogurt, plus more to serve
2 tbsp nutritional yeast
Cashew parmesan (see page 137) (optional)

FOR THE BEANS
1 tbsp extra virgin olive oil
1 large red onion, chopped
2 cloves garlic, sliced
1 tbsp smoked paprika
1 tsp cumin seeds
1 tin of chopped tomatoes
2 tbsp sun-dried tomato paste
1 tbsp soy sauce/tamari
1 tbsp rose harissa paste
250g (9oz) tinned white beans, drained
1 tsp maple syrup

Preheat your air fryer to 200°C (400°F) for 2 minutes.

Score the insides of the potatoes into a lattice shape. Rub the potatoes with the extra virgin olive oil and sprinkle with sea salt. Air fry in the basket for 15 minutes, then turn and cook for another 15 minutes. Check the centres are soft.

In the meantime, for the beans, put the extra virgin olive oil and onion in a wide-bottom pan and fry gently on a low heat for around 8 minutes until soft and browning. Add the garlic and spices and fry for 30 seconds more.

Add the tomatoes, sun-dried tomato paste, soy sauce and harissa to the pan and cook for 5–6 minutes.

Now add the beans and maple syrup and cook on a low heat for 5 minutes more. Finally, season well.

To serve, scoop out the centres of the potatoes and add the flesh to a bowl. Mash with a fork and stir in the yogurt and nutritional yeast. Season well and put back into the potato skins, then top with the beans, extra yogurt and the cashew parmesan (if using).

Smoky jackfruit sliders

Flavour-packed jackfruit, crunchy slaw and tangy gherkins in a
bun. Delicious! Cooking the jackfruit in the air fryer with the dressing
intensifies the flavours and makes it crispy without the need for frying.
Perfect for parties or family lunches.

SERVES 4
READY IN 20 MINUTES

1 tin of jackfruit, drained and
  shredded
3 tbsp soy sauce/tamari
1 tbsp hoisin sauce
1 tbsp balsamic glaze
1 tbsp sriracha
1 tbsp olive oil
1 tsp garlic granules

TO SERVE
4 buns of choice, halved
Slaw (see page 118)
Gherkins, sliced

Firstly, drain the jackfruit in a colander.

Place the jackfruit on a paper towel and pat it to
remove as much liquid as possible.

Transfer the jackfruit to a large bowl, then add all the
remaining dressing ingredients and stir to combine.
Season to taste.

Preheat the air fryer to 180°C (350°F) for 2 minutes.

Transfer the jackfruit mixture to a baking tin and air fry
for 12 minutes, stirring occasionally, until a little crispy.

Top the buns with smoky jackfruit, slaw and gherkins!

Roast pepper pesto & cheese toastie

Homemade roast pepper pesto and melty cheese in a toastie! Oh my goodness, this combination is AMAZING!!

SERVES 2
READY IN 20 MINUTES

FOR THE PESTO
4 red (bell) peppers, deseeded and sliced
Drizzle of olive oil
100g (1 cup) walnuts
4 tbsp nutritional yeast
1 small clove garlic, peeled
100g (¾ cup) sun-dried tomatoes in oil, drained
30g (1oz) fresh basil
2 tbsp extra virgin olive oil
50ml (scant ¼ cup) water

2 ciabatta rolls, sliced
1 tomato, sliced
2 tbsp mixed pitted olives, sliced
4 tbsp grated cheese or mozzarella

Preheat the air fryer to 200°C (400°F) for 2 minutes.

Put the red peppers, a drizzle of olive oil and some sea salt into the basket. Air fry for 7 minutes, until soft and charred.

To make the pesto, put the roast peppers and all the other ingredients into a food processor and blitz to combine.

To make the toasties, layer the pesto on the base of the rolls. Top with sliced tomato, olives and cheese. Add the tops of the rolls.

Place in the basket and air fry for 3 minutes, until the rolls are crispy and the cheese is melted.

Bombay potato toasted sandwich

If you love Indian flavours and a comforting toasted sandwich, this one is for you! Roast potatoes cooked in spices, then tossed in sticky onions, piled onto bread with a fresh mint dressing and toasted in the air fryer.

SERVES 2
READY IN 30 MINUTES

250 g (9 oz) potatoes, peeled and cut into 1cm (½ inch) cubes
1 tsp ground turmeric
1 tsp garam masala
2 tbsp olive oil
1 red onion, sliced into strips
1 tsp black mustard seeds
1 tsp cumin seeds
4 slices of fresh bread of choice

FOR THE MINT DRESSING
4 tbsp plain yogurt
Juice of ½ lemon
2 tbsp shredded fresh mint leaves
Pinch of chilli flakes

Preheat your air fryer to 180°C (350°F) for 2 minutes.

In a bowl, toss the chopped potatoes in the turmeric, garam masala, 1 tablespoon of the olive oil and some sea salt and black pepper. Add to a baking tin and air fry for 12 minutes, shaking occasionally.

In the meantime, cook the onion in the remaining oil in a saucepan for 6–7 minutes. Now add in the black mustard seeds and cumin seeds until they pop. Set aside.

To make the mint dressing, put everything in a jar and mix to combine. Season well.

To make each sandwich, combine the cooked potato and onion in a bowl and mash up a little.

Spread some mint dressing on both sides of a slice of bread, then add half the potato mix. Top with the second slice of bread, spread on both sides with mint dressing, then place in the air fryer.

Air fry on 200°C (400°F) for 3 minutes, until the bread is crispy and nicely browned.

Repeat to make the other sandwich.

SIMPLE LUNCHES & LIGHTER BITES

Loaded pea falafel pockets

A fun and tasty alternative to a classic falafel. Adding peas is both a delicious and budget-friendly option. You can load the pittas with anything you fancy, but I love creamy hummus, lots of salad and a big drizzle of sweet chilli sauce. The falafels are also great for tasty packed lunches.

SERVES 4
READY IN 25 MINUTES

200g (scant 1½ cups) frozen peas, defrosted

80g (3oz) tinned chickpeas (garbanzos)

1 tsp garlic powder

Juice of ½ lemon

10g (¼oz) fresh mint

40g (1½oz) bread of choice, toasted and crumbled

Oil spray

4 pittas

Hummus

Salad (leaves, sliced red onion, tomatoes)

Sweet chilli sauce

Put the peas, chickpeas, garlic powder, lemon juice and mint into a food processor and blitz until a rough paste is formed.

Add to a large bowl and mix in the breadcrumbs. Season to taste.

Preheat the air fryer to 180°C (350°F) for 2 minutes.

Spray a little oil onto a baking tin. Scoop up and shape small flat rounds of the falafel mixture, then add to the baking tin. Spray them with a little more oil.

Air fry for 5 minutes, then flip and cook for a further 2 minutes. Repeat with any remaining falafel mixture.

To serve, toast and split the pittas, then load them with hummus, salad, the pea falafels and sweet chilli sauce.

Roast Potatoes & Courgettes

with garlicky green yogurt

A fresh and tasty roast new potato salad with an incredible creamy pea tzatziki. This dish is perfect for a light dinner.

SERVES 4
READY IN 35 MINUTES

750g (1lb 10oz) baby potatoes, halved if large

3 tbsp extra virgin olive oil, plus more for drizzling

1 courgette (zucchini), sliced

Small bunch of asparagus, trimmed

Fresh mint/dill, chopped

FOR THE PEA TZATZIKI

200g (7oz) cucumber (approx. ½)

120g (scant 1 cup) frozen peas, defrosted

150g (generous ½ cup) plain yogurt

2 tbsp chopped fresh dill

1 tbsp chopped fresh mint

Juice of ½ lemon

1 clove garlic, minced

Preheat your air fryer to 200°C (400°F) for 2 minutes.

Toss the potatoes in 1 tablespoon of the extra virgin olive oil and some sea salt. Place the potatoes in the basket and air fry for 10 minutes. Shake the potatoes and cook until the potatoes are golden and tender – about 10 minutes more.

Remove and now add the courgette and asparagus to the baking tin with 1 tablespoon of the olive oil and some sea salt. Air fry for 6–8 minutes, shaking occasionally.

For the tzatziki, grate the cucumber and pop it into a large sieve to drain over a bowl. Squeeze out as much moisture as possible and transfer to a large bowl.

Crush the peas in another bowl. Add the peas and all the other ingredients to the cucumber and season, then add the remaining olive oil and mix well.

To serve, layer the tzatziki, roast potatoes, asparagus and courgette on plates. Top with fresh mint or dill and drizzle over some more extra virgin olive oil.

super
quick
meals

ready in 15 minutes or less

SO SPEEDY

Cheat's pizza
with pesto & mushrooms

Pizza in a flash? Look no further! This delicious wrap pizza makes a brilliant speedy lunch and kids will love it. You can, of course, add any toppings you fancy.

SERVES 1
READY IN 15 MINUTES

1 wrap of choice
3 mushrooms, sliced
50g (½ cup) grated cheese

FOR THE TOMATO SAUCE
2 tbsp sun-dried tomato paste
3 tbsp passata
1 tsp dried oregano
½ tsp pul biber chilli flakes/ smoked paprika

FOR THE PESTO
70g (½ cup) pine nuts, toasted
30g (1oz) fresh basil leaves
4 tbsp extra virgin olive oil
1 clove garlic, peeled
4 tbsp nutritional yeast
½ tsp sea salt
Juice of ½ lemon
50ml (scant ¼ cup) water

Preheat your air fryer to 200°C (400°F) for 2 minutes.

To make the tomato sauce, mix all the ingredients in a jar to combine.

To make the pesto, add all the ingredients to a food processor and blitz to combine.

To make the pizza, place the wrap in the basket. Load the wrap with the tomato sauce, mushrooms, pesto and grated cheese.

Air fry for 7–9 minutes, until the base is crispy and the cheese is melted. Garnish with fresh herb sprigs.

Sweet chilli crispy tofu bites

with dipping sauce

Sweet, salty, sticky tofu – a delicious high-protein snack, which can be whipped up in 10 minutes! Serve with dipping sauce for an extra treat.

SERVES 2
READY IN 10 MINUTES

300g (10½oz) smoked firm tofu, pressed
3 tbsp soy sauce/tamari
2 tbsp toasted sesame oil
2 tbsp sweet chilli sauce
Sesame seeds

FOR THE DIPPING SAUCE
2 tbsp soy sauce/tamari
1 tbsp rice vinegar
2 tbsp toasted sesame oil
2 tbsp sweet chilli sauce
Juice of ½ lime

Preheat your air fryer to 200°C (400°F) for 2 minutes.

Roughly break up the tofu into large chunks and add to a bowl.

Mix the soy sauce, toasted sesame oil and sweet chilli sauce in a jar, then add to the tofu. Mix to combine.

Transfer to a baking tin and air fry for 5 minutes, or until browned on the edges. Flip and cook for another 4 minutes.

To make the dipping sauce, mix the ingredients in a jar.

To serve, sprinkle the crispy tofu with sesame seeds and dip in the sauce.

Harissa garlic bread bruschetta

Speedy garlic bread with a difference – adding harissa makes it taste next-level delicious. The garlic butter melts and oozes into the bread whilst it toasts at the same time. Perfect for parties, serve with tomatoes and basil for a taste of summer.

SERVES 4
READY IN 10 MINUTES

4 slices of fresh bread
Chopped cherry tomatoes
Balsamic glaze
Fresh basil leaves

FOR THE GARLIC BUTTER
2 tbsp butter, at room
   temperature
1 tsp dried oregano
2 tbsp rose/standard harissa
   paste
3 cloves garlic, crushed

Preheat your air fryer to 200°C (400°F) for 2 minutes.

Mix all the garlic butter ingredients together in a small bowl. Spread the mix over the bread slices.

Place in a baking tin and air fry for 3–5 minutes.

Top with the chopped tomatoes, a drizzle of balsamic glaze and some fresh basil leaves. Eat straight away.

Spicy hummus

Making hummus is super easy and it's even better with herby croutons to scoop it all up with! Adding the ice cubes makes the hummus super creamy. Butter beans work well as an alternative to chickpeas.

SERVES 4
READY IN 15 MINUTES

1 tin of chickpeas
(garbanzos), drained
Juice of ½ lemon
1 tsp ground cumin
1 clove garlic, peeled
1 tsp harissa paste
½ tsp paprika
2 tbsp extra virgin olive oil,
plus more for drizzling
2 tbsp tahini
2 ice cubes (optional)

FOR THE CRISPY
CHICKPEAS
½ tsp ground cumin
1 tsp smoked paprika
½ tsp ground turmeric
1 tsp garlic granules
1 tin of chickpeas
(garbanzos), drained
1 tbsp extra virgin olive oil

FOR THE HERBY
CROUTONS
2 ciabatta rolls, cut into slices
1 tbsp olive oil
1 tsp dried oregano

Preheat your air fryer to 200°C (400°F) for 2 minutes.

To make the hummus, put all the ingredients in a food processor or high-speed blender and blitz for 1–2 minutes until very smooth and creamy. Season well.

To make the crispy chickpeas, put the spices, chickpeas and extra virgin olive oil in a baking tin.

Air fry for 6 minutes, until warm and crispy. Season well and set aside.

To make the croutons, put the bread in a bowl with the olive oil and oregano and toss to combine.

Add to the basket and air fry for 2 minutes.

To serve, top the hummus with the crispy chickpeas and a drizzle of extra virgin olive oil. Scoop up with the herby croutons.

Mushroom souvlaki wraps

Gorgeous flavours reminiscent of Greece here. A mouthwatering meal in minutes – very tasty indeed!

SERVES 2
READY IN 15 MINUTES

300g (10½oz) button mushrooms
2 flatbreads
Plain yogurt, mixed with a little lemon juice and sea salt
Red onion, cut into strips
1 tomato, chopped
Fresh mint leaves, shredded

FOR THE MARINADE
1 tbsp olive oil
2 tbsp soy sauce/tamari
1 tbsp balsamic glaze
1 tsp dried oregano
2 tsp dried mint
1 tsp garlic granules
2 tbsp sun-dried tomato paste

Put all the marinade ingredients in a large bowl and mix to combine. Season to taste.

Transfer the mushrooms to the bowl and coat thoroughly with the marinade.

Preheat your air fryer to 180°C (350°F) for 2 minutes.

Transfer the mushrooms to the basket and air fry for 3 minutes.

To serve, top the flatbreads with yogurt, mushrooms, onion, tomato and lots of fresh mint.

SUPER QUICK MEALS

Roast green veg toasted sandwich

Healthy but definitely not lacking in flavour! The tasty pea dip adds some plant-based protein and the courgette and roast broccoli give lots of crunch. Perfect for lunch or brunch.

SERVES 2
READY IN 10 MINUTES

1 small courgette (zucchini), thinly sliced
½ head of broccoli, sliced into small florets
Oil spray
4 slices of fresh bread
4 tbsp hummus
Olive oil

FOR THE PEA DIP
300g (10½oz) frozen peas, defrosted
15g (½oz) fresh mint, finely chopped
1 tsp Dijon mustard
1 clove garlic, peeled
Pinch of sea salt
2 tbsp olive oil

Preheat your air fryer to 200°C (400°F) for 2 minutes.

Put the courgette and broccoli in a baking tin, spray with oil and season. Air fry for 6 minutes, until cooked through and the broccoli is slightly charred.

Make the pea dip by putting all the ingredients into a food processor and blitzing to a chunky paste.

Make the sandwiches by loading two slices of bread with the pea dip, then top with the courgette and broccoli.

Spread the hummus on the other two slices of bread and make two sandwiches.

Add the first one to a baking tin and brush the top with olive oil. Air fry for 2 minutes, until crispy. Repeat with the other sandwich.

Courgette asparagus pesto tart

This puff pastry tart can be made in 15 minutes thanks to speedily cooking the base in the air fryer. I love to serve this with a big salad and olives. Some other topping ideas are roast veg, tomatoes and basil, red pesto and cheese.

SERVES 2
READY IN 15 MINUTES

1 sheet of ready-rolled puff pastry
1 shallot, thinly sliced
1 tbsp olive oil
¼ courgette (zucchini), thinly sliced
8 small asparagus spears, trimmed

FOR THE PESTO
70g (½ cup) pine nuts, toasted
30g (1oz) fresh basil leaves
4 tbsp extra virgin olive oil
1 clove garlic, peeled
4 tbsp nutritional yeast
½ tsp sea salt
Juice of ½ lemon
50ml (scant ¼ cup) water

Preheat your air fryer to 200°C (400°F) for 2 minutes.

Lightly oil a baking tin.

Cut the puff pastry out to fit the base of the baking tin, then cut out a long strip and place around the edge of the pastry base. Press a fork over the edge, pressing down to seal.

Air fry for 4 minutes, then flip and cook for another 3–4 minutes, until the pastry is crisp and golden.

Meanwhile, to make the pesto, add all the ingredients to a food processor and blitz to combine.

In a small pan, fry the shallot in the olive oil for 2–3 minutes, then add the courgette and asparagus. Fry for a few more minutes until soft. Season well.

To serve, top the crisp tart base with the pesto and sautéed vegetables.

Sticky mushroom burgers

These burgers can be whipped up in minutes and you get a lovely crispy outside and gooey inside. Absolutely brilliant served with some wedges and slaw. Be warned, these are incredibly addictive!

SERVES 2
READY IN 10 MINUTES

2 flat mushrooms
Hummus
2 ciabatta rolls, sliced
Sliced tomatoes
Grated cheese
Handful of salads leaves
   (optional)
Mayo

FOR THE MARINADE
2 tbsp olive oil
2 tbsp soy sauce/tamari
2 tbsp sun-dried tomato
   paste
1 tbsp balsamic glaze
1 tbsp smoked paprika
1 tsp dried oregano
1 tsp ground cumin

Put all the marinade ingredients in a large bowl and mix to combine. Transfer the mushrooms to the bowl and coat thoroughly.

Preheat your air fryer to 180°C (350°F) for 2 minutes.

Transfer the mushrooms to a baking tin and air fry for 3 minutes. Remove and slice the mushrooms.

Spread the hummus on the base of the rolls, top with the tomatoes and cheese and then with the mushroom slices. Add salad leaves, if you like. Spread mayo on the top of the rolls and sandwich together.

Add to the basket and air fry on 200°C (400°F) for 2 minutes. Slice and eat!

30-minute meals

SO EASY

Cheesy black bean quesadillas

Cooking in the air fryer means you can have roast veg in super-fast time and you get a gooey inside and crispy outside. I've used garlic mayo here, but standard works well also.

SERVES 4
READY IN 25 MINUTES

300g (10½oz) sweet potatoes, peeled and cut into small cubes
1 red (bell) pepper, deseeded and cut into cubes
1 tbsp extra virgin olive oil
1 tbsp fajita seasoning
2 tbsp garlic mayo
2 tortilla wraps
Oil spray

FOR THE BEAN MIX
1 tin of black beans, drained
4 tbsp sun-dried tomato paste
1 tbsp fajita seasoning
Juice of ½ lime
70g (¾ cup) grated cheese

Preheat your air fryer to 180°C (350°F) for 2 minutes.

Put the sweet potato and red pepper cubes onto a baking tin, drizzle over the extra virgin olive oil and sprinkle on the fajita seasoning, then air fry for 12–15 minutes, shaking occasionally.

For the bean mix, put all the ingredients in a bowl and mix to combine. Add the cooked potato and pepper and mix.

To make each quesadilla, spread half the garlic mayo over a wrap, then spoon half of the potato/pepper mix onto one side. Fold over and press down firmly. Cut in half. Repeat with the other wrap.

Add to the baking tin, spray with oil or brush a little extra oil over the top. Cook in batches, if necessary, for 3 minutes per slice.

Spicy bean burgers

I've left some whole beans for added texture here, which makes all the difference, I think. It's better to make these into small burgers so that they hold together well. You might need to add two per bun.

MAKES ABOUT
 10 BURGERS
READY IN 25 MINUTES

FOR THE BURGERS
1 tin of red kidney beans, rinsed
1 tin of chickpeas (garbanzos), rinsed and drained
1 tsp ground cumin
2 tsp garam masala
½ tsp garlic powder
3 tbsp chopped fresh coriander (cilantro)
4 tbsp sweet chilli sauce
2 tbsp sriracha
50g (¾ cup) fresh breadcrumbs

Oil spray
5 buns of choice, halved
Mayo
Little Gem lettuce leaves
Sliced tomatoes
Hummus

In a large bowl, mash (with a masher or your hands) the beans and chickpeas into a rough paste, leaving some of the beans and chickpeas whole. Now add all the remaining ingredients and mix to combine.

Preheat the air fryer to 180°C (350°F) for 2 minutes.

Spray a baking tin with a little oil. Scoop up golf ball-sized amounts of the mix and squeeze and shape in your hands to form small balls. Flatten and place in the tin. Spray with a little oil.

Air fry for 5 minutes, then flip and cook for 3 more minutes. Repeat with any remaining mixture.

To serve, top the buns with mayo, lettuce, the bean burgers, tomato slices and hummus. Replace the bun tops.

Spicy tofu noodles

This spicy little number rivals a takeaway and can be whipped up in less than 20 minutes. Adding the Korean chilli paste gochujang is a shortcut to incredible taste.

SERVES 4
READY IN 20 MINUTES

1 red onion, cut into half moons

1 tbsp coconut oil

200g (7oz) white cabbage, shredded

4 cloves garlic, sliced

1 thumb of fresh ginger, peeled and grated

200g (8oz) rice noodles

6 tbsp mixed roasted cashews and peanuts

Fresh coriander (cilantro)/ mint leaves, chopped

FOR THE CRISPY TOFU

3 tbsp toasted sesame oil

2 tbsp gochujang/sriracha

3 tbsp soy sauce/tamari

300g (10½oz) firm tofu, pressed and cut into medium-sized cubes

FOR THE SAUCE

2 tbsp gochujang/sriracha

3 tbsp soy sauce/tamari

Juice of ½ lime

3 tbsp toasted sesame oil

2 tbsp maple syrup

Preheat your air fryer to 200°C (400°F) for 2 minutes.

For the crispy tofu, mix the marinade ingredients in a large bowl, add the cubed tofu and toss to coat.

Transfer to your basket in a single layer and air fry for 5 minutes, or until browned on the edges. Flip and cook for another 4 minutes. Repeat if cooking in batches.

In the meantime, add the onion and coconut oil to a frying pan. Cook the onion for 7–8 minutes, then add the cabbage, garlic and ginger. Fry for 2–3 minutes until the cabbage is soft.

Cook the rice noodles according to the pack instructions, then drain.

Add all the sauce ingredients to the frying pan along with the noodles and tofu. Mix to combine.

Add the spicy tofu noodles to bowls and top with the roasted nuts and herbs.

Bean balls in puttanesca sauce

This is great served with pasta or crusty bread or turned into bean ball subs (my favourite). You could cook the tomato sauce in the air fryer if preferred, but in the interests of time, it makes sense to cook in a pan at the same time.

SERVES 4
READY IN 30 MINUTES

FOR THE BEAN BALLS
1 tin of black beans, rinsed and drained
1 tsp garlic powder
1 tsp smoked paprika
1 tbsp sun-dried tomato paste
1 tsp dried oregano
40g (scant ½ cup) oats of choice/rolled oats
Oil spray

FOR THE PUTTANESCA SAUCE
1 tbsp olive oil
1 red onion, chopped
4 cloves garlic, sliced
1 tsp smoked paprika
Pinch of chilli flakes
1 tsp dried oregano
4 tomatoes, chopped
2 tbsp sun-dried tomato paste
75ml (⅓ cup) water
4 tbsp pitted olives
2 tbsp capers, drained

To make the bean balls, put all the ingredients except the oil spray in a food processor and blitz until a rough paste is formed. Season to taste.

Preheat the air fryer to 180°C (350°F) for 2 minutes.

Spray a baking tin with a little oil. Scoop up golf ball-sized amounts of the mix and squeeze and roll in your hands to form balls. Place in the tin (don't overcrowd) and spray with a little oil.

Air fry for 5 minutes, then flip and cook for 2 more minutes. Repeat with the remaining mix.

In the meantime, for the sauce, put the olive oil and onion in a large frying pan and fry on a medium heat for about 8–10 minutes until soft and browning. Add in the garlic and stir for another few minutes, then add the spices and oregano, chopped tomatoes, sun-dried tomato paste and the water, stir, then cover and simmer for 10 minutes.

Season to taste and add in the olives and capers.

To serve, add the bean balls to the tomato sauce and stir to combine. Serve with crusty bread or pasta.

Sticky sesame tofu tacos & slaw

A feast of flavours here! Sticky Asian tofu, mashed avocado and a fresh herby slaw, all served on soft warm tacos. Perfect party food. You could swap the tofu for sweet potatoes or (bell) peppers.

SERVES 4
READY IN 30 MINUTES

300g (10½oz) firm tofu, pressed and cut into 2cm (¾ inch) cubes

Oil spray

1 large red onion, cut into strips

1 tbsp olive oil

3 cloves garlic, finely chopped

1–2 tbsp peeled and grated fresh ginger

Pinch of chilli flakes

5 tbsp soy sauce/tamari

1 tbsp toasted sesame oil

1 tbsp maple syrup

Juice of 1 lime

1 ripe avocado

4 soft tacos

FOR THE SLAW

¼ white cabbage, shredded

3 spring onions (scallions), sliced

20g (⅓ cup) chopped fresh mint/coriander (cilantro)

3 tbsp plain yogurt

Juice of ½ lime

Preheat your air fryer to 200°C (400°F) for 2 minutes.

Transfer the tofu cubes, sprayed with some oil, to the basket and air fry for 5 minutes, or until browned on the edges. Flip and cook for another 7 minutes.

While the tofu is cooking, fry the onion in the olive oil in a frying pan for 5–6 minutes. Add the garlic, ginger and chilli flakes and fry for a further minute.

Pour in the soy sauce, toasted sesame oil, maple syrup and half the lime juice. Cook on a medium heat for 2 minutes. Now add the cooked tofu, toss and season to taste.

Mash the avocado in a bowl with the remaining lime juice and season to taste.

To make the slaw, put the cabbage, spring onions, herbs, yogurt and lime juice in a large bowl. Mix well and season to taste.

To serve, heat the tacos according to the pack instructions and then top with the sticky tofu, avocado and crunchy slaw.

Lemon cauliflower

with sesame flatbread

Did you know you can cook flatbreads in an air fryer? My easy yogurt flatbreads puff up beautifully. Topped with speedy roast cauliflower and creamy hummus, this is simple but delicious.

SERVES 2
READY IN 20 MINUTES

1 small cauliflower, cut into small florets
2 tbsp extra virgin olive oil
Juice of ½ lemon
1 tsp garlic powder
4 tbsp hummus
Fresh coriander (cilantro)/ mint/dill

FOR THE FLATBREADS
100g (⅔ cup) self-raising flour, plus extra for dusting
75g (¼ cup) plain yogurt
2 tbsp extra virgin olive oil
1 tbsp sesame seeds, toasted

Preheat the air fryer to 180°C (350°F) for 2 minutes.

Put the cauliflower, extra virgin olive oil, lemon juice, garlic powder and some sea salt and black pepper in a baking tin. Air fry the cauliflower for 7–9 minutes (depending on the size of your florets).

To make the flatbreads, put the flour, yogurt, 1 tablespoon of the extra virgin olive oil and some sea salt in a large bowl. Stir until it comes together, then transfer to a floured board.

Knead for a few minutes until you get a springy dough, then divide the dough in half and roll out two flatbreads. Rub each with the remaining olive oil and sprinkle with toasted sesame seeds.

Air fry on 200°C (400°F) for 4 minutes, either using a dual fryer to add both flatbreads or cooking one at a time.

To serve, top the flatbreads with the hummus, lemon cauliflower and fresh herbs.

Roasted roots & butter bean salad

A salad suitable for all seasons. The roasted root vegetables make it a bit heartier, so it's perfect for autumn or even winter. The butter beans and seeds add delicious plant-based protein.

SERVES 2
READY IN 25 MINUTES

2 large carrots, thinly sliced
2 parsnips, sliced
2 red onions, quartered
1 tbsp extra virgin olive oil
1 tin of butter beans, drained
50g (1½ cups) rocket
3 tbsp sunflower seeds, toasted

FOR THE DRESSING
3 tbsp apple cider vinegar
2 tsp wholegrain mustard
1 tsp maple syrup
2 tbsp extra virgin olive oil

Preheat the air fryer to 180°C (350°F) for 2 minutes.

In a bowl, toss the carrots, parsnips and onions in the extra virgin olive oil and some sea salt. Place into the basket and air fry for 13–15 minutes, shaking every few minutes.

To make the dressing, pour the apple cider vinegar, mustard, maple syrup and extra virgin olive oil into a jar and mix to combine. Season to taste.

To serve, toss together the roast veg, butter beans, rocket, dressing and sunflower seeds.

Charred cabbage
with harissa lentils & lemon yogurt

If you haven't tried charred cabbage, you're in for a treat! It's completely transformed by roasting it until crispy. It's best to use a dual air fryer here, but if you don't have one, just cook in batches.

SERVES 4
READY IN 20 MINUTES

2 red (bell) peppers, deseeded and chopped
2 tbsp olive oil
1 small pointed cabbage or ½ a large one
1 tbsp balsamic vinegar

FOR THE HARISSA LENTILS
240g (8½oz) precooked green lentils, rinsed
1 red onion, finely chopped
100g (⅔ cup) cherry tomatoes, chopped
50g (½ cup) walnuts, toasted and crushed a little
Big handful of fresh mint/dill, chopped
1–2 tbsp harissa paste
2 tbsp extra virgin olive oil

FOR THE LEMON YOGURT
Juice of ½ lemon
4 tbsp plain yogurt

Preheat the air fryer to 200°C (400°F) for 2 minutes.

To cook the red peppers, place in the basket, drizzle with 1 tablespoon of the olive oil and some sea salt. Air fry for about 7 minutes.

To cook the cabbage, slice the cabbage in half (through the root so it holds together), then in half again. Put in the other basket with the remaining 1 tablespoon of olive oil, some sea salt and the balsamic vinegar.

Air fry cut-side down on 180°C (350°F) for 6 minutes, then flip and cook for another 6 minutes.

For the harissa lentils, in a large bowl, mix together the roast peppers, lentils and all the other ingredients. Season well.

For the lemon yogurt, mix the lemon juice and yogurt in a small bowl. Season to taste.

Serve the cabbage with the lentils and lemon yogurt.

Cauliflower steaks
with romesco sauce & chickpeas

I love a roast cauliflower! This is a light and healthy meal on its own, but I also like to serve it with crispy potatoes. The romesco sauce can also be used like pesto and it's great with pasta, roast veg or on toast. A dual air fryer is recommended for the cauliflower and peppers.

SERVES 2
READY IN 25 MINUTES

1 cauliflower, sliced into steaks

3 tbsp extra virgin olive oil

1 tin of chickpeas (garbanzos), drained

20g (⅓ cup) chopped mixed fresh dill and mint

FOR THE ROMESCO SAUCE

3 red (bell) peppers, deseeded and chopped

50ml (scant ¼ cup) extra virgin olive oil

50g (½ cup) ground almonds (almond meal)

2 tbsp sun-dried tomato paste

1 clove garlic, peeled

1 tbsp smoked paprika

4 tbsp red wine vinegar

Preheat the air fryer to 180°C (350°F) for 2 minutes.

To cook the red peppers, place in the basket, drizzle with 1 tablespoon of the extra virgin olive oil and some sea salt and black pepper. Air fry for about 10 minutes, shaking occasionally.

Put the cauliflower in the other basket along with 1 tablespoon of the olive oil and season well. Air fry on 180°C (350°F) for 7 minutes, then flip the steaks around and cook for 5 more minutes.

To make the sauce, put all the ingredients, along with the roast peppers, in a food processor and blitz together to combine.

For the chickpeas, mix the chickpeas, herbs and remaining 1 tablespoon of olive oil in a bowl. Season well.

Serve the cauliflower steaks on a bed of romesco sauce and top with the chickpeas.

Roasted squash ragu

Slicing the squash lengthways here helps with the cooking process. The final step of adding it back to the air fryer and topping with cheese is optional but delicious. I've cooked this in a large-capacity air fryer. If cooked in a smaller version, you may need to cook the squash in batches.

SERVES 4
READY IN 30 MINUTES

1 small squash, peeled, deseeded and cut into 8 segments lengthways

Oil spray

1 red onion, finely chopped

2 tbsp olive oil

4 cloves garlic, sliced

1 large carrot, finely chopped

200g (scant 1½ cups) cherry tomatoes, roughly chopped

50ml (scant ¼ cup) white wine

2 tbsp tomato purée

250ml (1 cup) vegetable stock

250g (9oz) precooked Puy lentils, rinsed

1 tbsp fresh thyme leaves

1 tbsp balsamic vinegar

20–30g (⅓ cup) grated cheese

Preheat the air fryer to 180°C (350°F) for 2 minutes.

Slice across the squash segments along the length (make sure you don't go all the way through). Spray the air fryer basket with some oil spray.

Place the squash in the basket in a single layer, spray with oil, season and air fry for 10 minutes, then turn and cook for a further 10 minutes.

In the meantime, in a large pan, fry the onion in the olive oil for 6–7 minutes until soft.

Add the garlic and carrot and fry for 2–3 minutes.

Now add the tomatoes and white wine, stir to combine and fry for a further 2–3 minutes. Finally, add in the tomato purée, stock, lentils, thyme and balsamic. Simmer for 6–7 minutes until the tomatoes have softened. Season well.

Finally, remove the air fryer basket and spoon the lentil mixture into the base of the air fryer.

Add the roasted squash and top with the grated cheese. Air fry on 200°C (400°F) for 3 minutes, until the cheese has all melted.

Peas & greens mac 'n' cheese

Mac 'n' cheese with a difference. I've added lots of peas and cabbage greens for some healthy additions. Cooking this in an air fryer means it's ready in super-quick time for a speedy family dinner. This can be cooked in a baking tin that fits inside your air fryer or just added to the base of the air fryer and scooped out to serve. I cooked this in a large-capacity air fryer.

SERVES 4–6
READY IN 25 MINUTES

270g (1¾ cups) macaroni
3 tbsp butter
4 tbsp plain flour
200ml (generous ¾ cup) milk
250ml (1 cup) vegetable stock made with 1 bouillon cube
1 tbsp white miso paste
1 tsp smoked paprika
1 tsp garlic granules
150g (1½ cups) grated smoked cheese
200g (scant 1½ cups) frozen peas
80g (3oz) cabbage greens, chopped

Cook the macaroni according to the pack instructions and drain.

To make the cheesy béchamel sauce, add the butter to a saucepan and melt on a low heat, then add the flour. Stir to combine well.

Next, add the milk, stock, miso, paprika and garlic granules. Simmer for 5 minutes, stirring constantly to ensure no lumps form. Add 100g (1 cup) of the smoked cheese and stir well.

Now add the peas and cabbage greens and stir to combine, then cook for 1–2 minutes. Add the drained pasta straight into the sauce and stir through.

Preheat your air fryer to 180°C (350°F) for 2 minutes.

Transfer the mac 'n' cheese into the base of your air fryer or into a large baking tin that fits your air fryer and sprinkle over the remaining smoked cheese.

Air fry for 10 minutes, until bubbling and crispy on top.

Easy tomato & lentil pasta

An easy pasta dish. Just fry up some onion and garlic, then add everything to your air fryer and let it cook away to make a tasty sauce. This is great as it is but even better topped with cashew Parmesan for the important 'cheesy' flavour.

SERVES 4
READY IN 25 MINUTES

1 red onion, sliced

1 tbsp olive oil

4 cloves garlic, sliced

6 tomatoes, chopped

250g (9oz) precooked Puy lentils, rinsed

1 tbsp smoked paprika

1 tsp dried oregano

100ml (scant ½ cup) vegetable stock

3 tbsp sun-dried tomato paste

250g (9oz) pasta of choice

Cashew parmesan (see page 137)

Firstly, put your onion and olive oil in a frying pan and fry gently on a low heat for around 7–8 minutes until soft and browning. Add the garlic and fry for a further minute.

Preheat the air fryer to 180°C (350°F) for 2 minutes.

Transfer the onion and garlic, along with the chopped tomatoes, lentils, paprika, oregano, stock and sun-dried tomato paste to the base of the air fryer. Air fry for 15–20 minutes.

Meanwhile, cook the pasta according to the pack instructions and drain.

To serve, toss the pasta and sauce together. Top with the fresh herbs and cashew parmesan.

Baked sweet potato carbonara

A delicious carbonara made with roast sweet potato (although you'd never know it). Two things really elevate this dish – the lemon zest and baking it with a cheesy nutty breadcrumb topping!

SERVES 4
READY IN 30 MINUTES

1 large sweet potato, peeled and cubed (about 450g/1lb)
Oil spray
250g (9oz) spaghetti or other pasta of choice
250ml (1 cup) oat milk
3 tbsp nutritional yeast
150ml (generous ½ cup) vegetable stock
1 tbsp white miso paste
1 tbsp apple cider vinegar
Zest of 1 lemon
100g (¾ cup) grated cheese (vegan melty)
30g (½ cup) fresh breadcrumbs
2 tbsp crushed hazelnuts

Preheat your air fryer to 180°C (350°F) for 2 minutes.

Put the sweet potato in the basket and spray over some oil on its own or with some sea salt. Air fry for about 12 minutes, shaking occasionally until cooked.

Cook the pasta according to the pack instructions, then drain and return to the saucepan.

To make the sauce, put the roasted sweet potato, milk, nutritional yeast, stock, miso and apple cider vinegar in a food processor. Blitz until you get a creamy sauce. Add a little water for a looser consistency, then transfer to the saucepan with the drained pasta.

Grate in the lemon zest, stir to combine, then transfer the pasta mixture to a cake tin or high-sided baking tray that fits in your air fryer.

Mix the grated cheese, breadcrumbs and hazelnuts in a bowl. Top the pasta and place in the air fryer. Air fry on 200°C (400°F) for 5–6 minutes until the top is crunchy.

Crispy gnocchi
with cherry tomatoes

Have you tried air-fried gnocchi? It becomes beautifully crispy on the outside and squidgy on the inside – so good! I've paired it with a super-fast tomato sauce and crunchy, 'cheesy' cashew parmesan.

SERVES 2
READY IN 30 MINUTES

1 red onion, sliced
2 tbsp olive oil
4 cloves garlic, sliced
250g (generous 1½ cups) cherry tomatoes, chopped
1 tsp dried oregano
2 tbsp sun-dried tomato paste
10g (¼oz) fresh basil leaves, shredded
1 pack of gnocchi

FOR THE CASHEW PARMESAN
75g (½ cup) cashews
2 tbsp nutritional yeast

To make the tomato sauce, put the onion and 1 tablespoon of olive oil in a saucepan and fry for 6–7 minutes until soft. Now add the garlic and fry for a further minute or so.

Add the tomatoes, oregano and tomato paste to the pan. Simmer and allow the tomatoes to break down for 2–3 minutes. Now add the basil and season to taste.

To make the cashew parmesan, add the cashews and nutritional yeast to a mini chopper or food processor with a pinch of sea salt and blitz to a chunky crumb.

To cook the gnocchi, preheat your air fryer to 200°C (400°F) for 2 minutes.

Toss the gnocchi in the remaining olive oil. Season with sea salt and black pepper. Transfer the gnocchi to the basket and air fry for 10 minutes, until crisp and golden, shaking occasionally.

To serve, toss the gnocchi in the tomato sauce and sprinkle with the cashew parmesan.

Courgette pesto pasta

A crowd-pleaser – pesto pasta with a twist. The roast courgettes add creaminess and the toasted breadcrumbs give a great texture. Keep any leftover pesto in the fridge to spread on toast or dollop into roast veg.

SERVES 2
READY IN 25 MINUTES

600g (1lb 5oz) courgettes (zucchini) (about 3), chopped into small cubes

4 tbsp extra virgin olive oil

1 ciabatta roll, roughly torn into pieces

100g (⅔ cup) pine nuts, plus 2 tbsp for the breadcrumbs

25g (41/2 oz) pasta of choice

30g (1oz) fresh basil leaves

1 tsp white miso paste

4 tbsp nutritional yeast

1 clove garlic, peeled

Juice of ½ lemon

Preheat your air fryer to 180°C (350°F) for 2 minutes.

To roast the courgettes, put the courgettes in a baking tin, drizzle with a little of the extra virgin olive oil and season well. Air fry for 15 minutes, shaking occasionally.

Set aside and cool a little, reserving 4 tablespoons to top the pasta.

Meanwhile, to make the nutty breadcrumbs, put the roll in a food processor and pulse until finely chopped. Add 2 tablespoons of the pine nuts and briefly pulse again.

Transfer to a small frying pan with 1 tablespoon of the extra virgin olive oil. Toast for 2–3 minutes until lightly browned. Add a little sea salt and set aside.

Cook the pasta according to the pack instructions and then drain.

To make the pesto, put the courgettes, the rest of the olive oil and all the remaining ingredients in your food processor and blitz to combine. Season to taste.

To serve, add the pesto to the pasta as desired. Top with the reserved courgettes and nutty breadcrumbs.

Cherry tomato roast veg pasta

Bursting with fresh, summery flavours, roasted cherry tomatoes and summer veg are blitzed into a simple but delicious sauce. Brilliant for all the family, and any leftovers make a great packed lunch.

SERVES 4
READY IN 25 MINUTES

400g (2⅔ cups) cherry tomatoes

1 courgette (zucchini), cut into small cubes

1 red (bell) pepper, deseeded and cut into small cubes

1 red onion, cut into strips

2 cloves garlic, sliced

2 tbsp olive oil

1 tbsp balsamic vinegar, plus more for drizzling

250g (9oz) pasta of choice

1 tsp dried oregano

30g (1oz) fresh basil leaves shredded

2 tbsp sun-dried tomato paste

2 tbsp nutritional yeast (optional)

Chilli flakes (optional), to garnish

Fresh basil leaves, to garnish

Preheat the air fryer to 180°C (350°F) for 2 minutes.

Add the vegetables, garlic, olive oil, some sea salt and black pepper and the balsamic to a baking tin and stir to combine.

Air fry for 10–12 minutes, shaking occasionally.

In the meantime, cook the pasta according to the pack instructions, then drain.

Reserve a quarter of the roast vegetables to top the pasta, then put the remaining veg in a saucepan along with their juices, the oregano, basil, tomato paste and nutritional yeast (if using) and blitz with an immersion blender to make a chunky sauce (or just blitz everything together in a food processor). Season well.

Add the sauce to the pasta and mix to combine.

To serve, top the pasta with the reserved roast veg, a drizzle of balsamic, some chilli flakes, if using, and fresh basil.

Creamy bhajis curry

I think you might like this one. A lovely tomato and coconut curry served with crispy onion bhajis! Making the bhajis in the air fryer is simple, fun and you get an amazing crispy result. Of course, you can eat them on their own as a snack too.

SERVES 2
READY IN 30 MINUTES

FOR THE BHAJIS
2 large red onions, sliced into strips
75g (½ cup) plain flour
1 tsp garam masala
1 tsp ground cumin
1 tsp ground turmeric
Pinch of chilli flakes
½ tsp sea salt
1 tbsp olive oil
50ml (scant ¼ cup) water
Oil spray

FOR THE CURRY
2 onions, roughly chopped
2 tbsp olive oil
3 cloves garlic, sliced
1 tsp cumin seeds
1 tsp ground coriander
½ tsp chilli flakes
1 tsp ground turmeric
4 ripe tomatoes, chopped
½ tin of coconut milk

To make the bhajis, add all the ingredients except the oil spray to a large mixing bowl.

Mix using your hands and then squeeze everything together while mixing until the onions release their moisture. The mix shouldn't be wet but thick and sticky.

Preheat your air fryer to 200°C (400°F) for 2 minutes.

Spray a little oil on the basket. Scoop up some batter, place onto the basket and flatten. Add more, but don't overcrowd. Spray with some more oil and air fry for 5 minutes. Flip and cook for 2–3 more minutes. Repeat with any remaining mixture.

In the meantime, fry the onion for the curry in the olive oil in a frying pan for approx. 8–10 minutes until soft and browning.

Add in the garlic and spices and stir for another minute, then add in the chopped tomatoes. Cook for a further 5–6 minutes, covered, stirring occasionally. Season to taste and stir in the coconut milk.

Blend the curry mixture with an immersion blender until smooth and creamy.

Serve the bhajis with the curry plus rice or flatbreads.

Red curry

A lovely red curry topped with crunchy veg. A dual air fryer is ideal here as you can cook the veg and curry at the same time. If you don't have one, you can either cook the veg in the air fryer and the curry in the pan with the leeks, or cook the veg first, then the curry in the air fryer.

SERVES 4
READY IN 30 MINUTES

1 carrot, sliced into batons

125g (4½oz) baby sweetcorn, halved lengthways

1 green (bell) pepper, deseeded and cut into strips

1 courgette (zucchini), sliced

1 tbsp olive oil

Roasted salted peanuts

FOR THE CURRY

2 leeks, trimmed and sliced

1 tbsp olive oil

2 cloves garlic, minced

1 knob of fresh ginger, peeled and grated

2 tbsp red curry paste

1 tin of coconut milk

1 tbsp peanut butter

2 tbsp soy sauce/tamari

1 tsp sugar

Juice of ½ lime

Preheat the air fryer to 180°C (350°F) for 2 minutes.

Place the veg in a baking tin, drizzle with the olive oil and season well. Air fry for about 10 minutes, or until tender, shaking occasionally.

In the meantime, for the curry, fry the leek in the olive oil in a pan for 7–8 minutes. Add the garlic and ginger and fry for a further minute.

Remove from the heat and transfer to the base of your air fryer along with all the remaining curry ingredients.

Stir to combine and air fry for 5–6 minutes.

To serve, top the curry with the crispy veg and some roasted salted peanuts and serve with rice.

Cauliflower, potato & pea curry

Roasting the veg adds tons of flavour! A dual air fryer is recommended here, but you can also cook the potatoes and cauliflower sequentially.

SERVES 2–4
READY IN 30 MINUTES

450g (1lb) baby potatoes, roughly chopped
2 tbsp olive oil
1 small cauliflower, cut into small florets

FOR THE CURRY
1 tbsp olive oil
1 large onion, roughly chopped
1 tsp cumin seeds
1 tsp ground turmeric
1 tsp garam masala
½–1 tsp chilli flakes
3 cloves garlic, sliced
1 thumb of fresh ginger, peeled and grated
6 tomatoes, roughly chopped
200g (scant 1½ cups) frozen peas
4–5 tbsp coconut yogurt/cream/plain yogurt

Preheat your air fryer to 200°C (400°F) for 2 minutes.

To roast the potatoes, toss them in 1 tablespoon of the olive oil and some sea salt.

Place the potatoes in the basket and air fry for 10 minutes. Shake the potatoes occasionally and cook until they are golden and tender – about 5 minutes.

To cook the cauliflower, toss the cauliflower in the remaining olive oil with some sea salt and black pepper and place in a baking tin. Air fry the cauliflower on 180°C (350°F) for 9–10 minutes.

In the meantime, for the curry, add the olive oil to a large frying pan with the onion. Fry the onion for about 8–10 minutes until soft and browning. Add in the spices and stir for a few minutes, then add in the garlic and ginger and stir for another few minutes.

Now add in the chopped tomatoes and cook on a medium heat for a further 5–6 minutes until the tomatoes have broken down a little.

You can now add the frozen peas and roast veg and stir in the coconut yogurt or cream. Season to taste and serve.

Tofu with peanut slaw

The crunchy slaw/salad here is simple yet absolutely delicious.
You could make this meal more substantial by adding some cooked
rice or noodles.

SERVES 2–4
READY IN 30 MINUTES

2 tbsp toasted sesame oil

3 tbsp sriracha

2 tbsp soy sauce/tamari

1 tbsp maple syrup

3 tbsp desiccated coconut

2 tbsp sesame seeds

400g (14oz) firm tofu, pressed
  and sliced into 8

FOR THE PEANUT SLAW

100g (⅓ cup) roasted salted
  peanuts, plus more to
  garnish

100g (3½oz) white cabbage,
  shredded

Handful of fresh coriander
  (cilantro) and mint leaves,
  plus more to garnish

2 carrots, shredded

3 spring onions (scallions),
  sliced

FOR THE DRESSING

1 tbsp sriracha

Juice of ½ lime

1 tbsp soy sauce/tamari

1 tsp maple syrup

3 tbsp mayo

Preheat the air fryer to 200°C (400°F) for 2 minutes.

To prepare the tofu steaks, mix the sesame oil, sriracha,
soy sauce and maple syrup in a small bowl.

Put the coconut and sesame seeds on a plate and mix.

Brush each tofu slice with the wet mix, then coat in the
coconut/sesame seeds. Place each slice in the basket,
adding as many as you can, but ensuring they're in a
single layer.

Air fry the tofu steaks for 4 minutes, then flip and cook
for another 4 minutes or until crispy. Repeat with the
remaining slices if needed.

To make the slaw, put all the ingredients in a large bowl
and toss to combine.

To make the dressing, add all the ingredients to a glass
jar and mix to combine.

To serve, add the dressing to the slaw and toss to
combine. Top the slaw with the tofu and the additional
peanuts and fresh herbs.

Roast squash tagine

This fragrant and vegetable-packed squash tagine is served with couscous and a tahini dressing. It's also super simple to make. I cooked this in a large-capacity air fryer.

SERVES 4
READY IN 30 MINUTES

200g (1 cup) couscous

1 medium squash, peeled, deseeded and cut into 1.5cm (⅝ inch) chunks (about 700g/1lb 9oz)

1 red (bell) pepper, deseeded and cut into thick strips

1 red onion, cut into 8 wedges

½ courgette (zucchini), sliced

1 tbsp olive oil

2 tbsp tagine paste/harissa paste

3 tbsp sun-dried tomato paste

500ml (2 cups) vegetable stock

100g (scant 1 cup) pitted green olives

1 tin of chickpeas (garbanzos), rinsed and drained

4 dried apricots, chopped

4 tbsp chopped fresh mint

FOR THE TAHINI SAUCE
Juice of ½ lemon
2 tbsp tahini
50ml (scant ¼ cup) water
2 tbsp extra virgin olive oil

Preheat your air fryer to 180°C (350°F) for 2 minutes.

Cook the couscous according to the pack instructions.

In a bowl, toss the squash, red pepper, onion and courgette with the olive oil and season well.

Transfer to the basket and air fry for about 15 minutes, shaking occasionally, until just tender.

Now remove the basket and transfer the vegetables to the base of the air fryer. Add the tagine paste, tomato paste, stock, olives, chickpeas and apricots.

Stir together well, then cook for another 10 minutes, stirring occasionally.

Finally, stir in the fresh mint and season to taste.

To make the tahini sauce, add all the ingredients to a jar and mix to combine.

Serve the tagine with the couscous and tahini sauce.

Tofu & chips

This is a fun recipe to make and a great one for the family. The tofu and peas are also delicious in a sandwich! You'll need a dual air fryer for this one.

SERVES 2–4
READY IN 30 MINUTES

3 tbsp soy sauce/tamari

2 tbsp sriracha

2 tbsp extra virgin olive oil

300g (10½oz) firm tofu, pressed and sliced into 12

500g (1lb 2oz) potatoes, cut into wedges

1 tsp garlic granules

100g (generous 1½ cups) fresh breadcrumbs

Oil spray

FOR THE PEA MASH

300g (2 cups) frozen peas, defrosted

1 gherkin

1 tbsp extra virgin olive oil

2 tbsp plain yogurt

Handful of fresh mint leaves

To prepare the tofu, put the soy sauce, sriracha and 1 tablespoon of the extra virgin olive oil in a bowl, add the tofu and gently coat. Leave to marinate for 10 minutes while the potatoes start cooking.

For the chips, preheat the air fryer to 180°C (350°F) for 2 minutes.

In another bowl, mix the potatoes, the remaining olive oil, some sea salt and black pepper and the garlic granules. Toss to combine. Lay out in a baking tin and air fry for 20 minutes, shaking a few times.

After 10 minutes, start to air fry the tofu in batches in another tin. Mix the breadcrumbs with some black pepper and a pinch of sea salt. Dip the tofu into the breadcrumbs and coat on all sides. Place each slice of breaded tofu in the baking tin as you go and when the tin is full, give the tofu a good spray of oil.

Air fry on 200°C (400°F) for 6–7 minutes, turning halfway through. Repeat with all the slices.

To make the pea mash, add all the ingredients to your food processor or blender. Blitz until you get a slightly chunky mash.

Serve the crusted tofu with the pea mash and chips.

Roast cauliflower satay & peas fried rice

Creamy, peanutty satay dressing, fried rice with peas and lovely crispy cauliflower – a heavenly and comforting combo of flavours. Broccoli also works well here.

SERVES 2
READY IN 25 MINUTES

1 medium cauliflower, cut into small florets
1 tbsp olive oil
½ tsp ground turmeric
250g (1⅓ cups) cooked rice
100g (⅔ cup) frozen peas
1 tbsp soy sauce/tamari
1 tbsp toasted sesame oil
Juice of ½ lime
Roasted salted peanuts
Fresh coriander (cilantro) leaves

FOR THE SATAY DRESSING
1 tbsp soy sauce/tamari
2 tbsp toasted sesame oil
½ tin of coconut milk
¼ tsp brown rice miso
3 tbsp smooth peanut butter
1 tbsp sriracha

Preheat the air fryer to 180°C (350°F) for 2 minutes.

Add the cauliflower florets to a baking tin with the olive oil, turmeric and some sea salt. Toss and air fry for 8 minutes, until crispy and cooked through.

Meanwhile, to make the satay dressing, put all the ingredients in a saucepan, stir and heat on a medium heat for 1–2 minutes.

To make the peas fried rice, put the cooked rice, peas, soy sauce, toasted sesame oil and lime juice in a frying pan and cook for 2–3 minutes, stirring occasionally.

To serve, top the peas fried rice with the roasted cauliflower and add lots of the satay dressing, roasted salted peanuts and fresh coriander.

Jerk veggie bowl

This veggie bowl is absolutely packed with flavour and it's super healthy with its fresh vegetables and protein-rich beans. The punchy jerk seasoning on the roast veg adds loads of flavour.

SERVES 2–4
READY IN 25 MINUTES

1 red (bell) pepper, deseeded and chopped

1 courgette (zucchini), chopped

2 carrots, chopped

2 tbsp jerk seasoning

1 tbsp olive oil

Plain yogurt

FOR THE BEANS & RICE

1 tbsp olive oil

2 spring onions (scallions), chopped

240g (8½oz) tinned black beans, drained

250g (9oz) cooked rice/ quinoa of choice

Juice of 1 lime

1 tbsp marmalade

½ ripe mango, peeled, stoned and cut into cubes

Big handful of fresh mint and coriander (cilantro), shredded

Preheat your air fryer to 180°C (350°F) for 2 minutes.

Toss the vegetables in the jerk seasoning and the olive oil and season well. Transfer to your basket and air fry for approx. 12 minutes, or until tender.

To make the beans and rice, add the olive oil to a frying pan with the spring onions. Fry for 4–5 minutes until soft, then add all the remaining ingredients apart from the mango and herbs and cook for 2–3 minutes.

Turn off the heat and mix the roast vegetables, mango and herbs into the rice. Serve each portion of rice with a spoonful of plain yogurt drizzled over.

bread, cakes, cookies & desserts

SWEET

Easy soda bread

I was so pleased to learn you can cook soda bread in your air fryer. Soda bread is one of the easiest breads to cook and it's even easier and more cost-effective to be able to cook it in your air fryer. The crust gets super crispy and delicious, whilst the inside is perfectly moist and dense like it should be.

SERVES 8
READY IN 30 MINUTES

200g (1⅓ cups) plain wholemeal flour

150 g (1 cup) plain white flour

1 tsp bicarbonate of soda (baking soda)

50g (½ cup) rolled oats, plus extra for sprinkling

1 tsp sea salt

250ml (1 cup) milk

1 tbsp apple cider vinegar

1 tsp maple syrup

75g (¼ cup) plain yogurt

Preheat the air fryer to 200°C (400°F) for 2 minutes.

Grease and flour a high-sided cake tin that fits inside the air fryer.

Mix all the dry ingredients together thoroughly in a large bowl. Add the milk, apple cider vinegar, maple syrup and yogurt and stir to combine.

Stir until you get a dough and then form into a ball. Place the ball in the floured cake tin and cut a deep cross in the centre. Sprinkle a few oats on the top.

Air fry for 10 minutes, then reduce the temperature to 180°C (350°F) and bake for a further 15 minutes.

Remove from the air fryer and allow to cool before slicing. Serve toasted with jam, marmalade or your favourite savoury toppings.

Easy flatbreads

Can you believe you can make flatbreads in the air fryer? It's so easy!
This is my classic flour and yogurt recipe, which is great plain but
even better brushed with a little extra virgin olive oil and topped with
sesame seeds for a nutty contrast.

MAKES 2 FLATBREADS
READY IN 15 MINUTES

100g (⅔ cup) self-raising
  flour, plus extra for dusting
75g (¼ cup) plain yogurt
1 tbsp olive oil
Oil spray
Extra virgin olive oil
Sesame seeds
Za'atar
Sea salt flakes
Hummus

In a large bowl, combine the flour, yogurt, olive oil and
a pinch of sea salt, stirring until it comes together, then
transfer to a floured board.

Knead for a few minutes until you get a springy dough.

Divide the dough in half, then roll out the first flatbread
on the board.

Preheat the air fryer to 200°C (400°F) for 2 minutes.

Spray the basket of the air fryer with oil spray. Rub each
flatbread with a little extra virgin olive oil and sprinkle
with sesame seeds, za'atar and sea salt flakes, if using.

Air fry for 4 minutes, flipping once. Repeat with the other
flatbread. These are delicious dipped into hummus.

Choc chip & pistachio cookies

I think you'll love these gorgeous little gooey cookies. They are moist and sweet with a great crust as they are cooked in the air fryer. These work best when cooked on baking paper with small holes in. You can buy this or make your own by piercing with a skewer.

MAKES 8–10 COOKIES
READY IN 25 MINUTES

50g (scant ¼ cup) butter, melted
1 tbsp milk
100g (⅔ cup) plain flour
50g (¼ cup) caster sugar
1 tsp vanilla extract
½ tsp bicarbonate of soda (baking soda)
50g (⅓ cup) dairy-free choc chips
25g (¼ cup) pistachios, crushed

Preheat the air fryer to 140°C (285°F) for 2 minutes.

In a large bowl, combine all the ingredients apart from the choc chips and nuts. Bring together to form a dough. Now add the choc chips and incorporate into the dough.

Scoop up 1 tablespoon at a time and form into a cookie shape. Add to the basket lined with baking paper and top with some crushed pistachios. Press down a little. Repeat with the remaining mix but don't overcrowd as the cookies will expand.

Air fry the cookies for 10 minutes, until crisp on the outside. Repeat with any remaining cookie mixture. Allow to cool on a wire rack.

Baked bananas

with caramel sauce

Baking the bananas in the air fryer makes them warm, gooey and caramelised. Combined with the caramel date sauce and some ice cream, it's a dream dessert.

SERVES 2
READY IN 15 MINUTES

2 ripe bananas, peeled and
    sliced lengthways
½ tsp ground cinnamon
1 tbsp brown/demerara sugar
Oil spray
Flaked almonds

FOR THE CARAMEL DATE
SAUCE
3 Medjool dates, pitted and
    finely chopped
150ml (generous ½ cup) milk
2 tbsp smooth peanut butter
½ tsp vanilla extract

Preheat the air fryer to 180°C (350°F) for 2 minutes.

Line a baking tin with baking paper and add the banana slices. Sprinkle with the cinnamon and sugar and spray with oil.

Air fry for 12 minutes, until the banana slices are golden and caramelised.

Meanwhile, to make the sauce, add all the ingredients to a saucepan with a pinch of sea salt and stir gently to heat through and thicken.

Serve the bananas with the caramel date sauce and a scattering of flaked almonds. Top each portion with a scoop of ice cream

Apple, peanut & date cake

A really lovely combination of flavours with the peanut butter, dates and apples. I love that it has lots of healthy ingredients, so you can feel semi-virtuous. You could, however, top with butter or cream for a more indulgent version.

SERVES 8
READY IN 30 MINUTES

100g (3½oz) Medjool dates, pitted
3 tbsp peanut butter
200ml (generous ¾ cup) milk
1 tsp vanilla extract
130g (scant 1 cup) plain flour
1 tsp ground cinnamon
1 tsp baking powder
1 medium eating apple, peeled, cored and chopped into 1cm (½ inch) cubes
½ eating apple, cored and cut into thin slices
Sugar

Preheat your air fryer to 150°C (300°F) for 2 minutes.

Put the dates, peanut butter, milk and vanilla extract in a food processor and blitz to a paste.

Mix the dry ingredients in a bowl.

Transfer the wet mix into the dry mix along with the cubed apple and mix to combine.

Line an 18cm (7 inch) shallow round metal baking tin with baking paper and spoon in the mixture. Top with the apple slices and sprinkle over some sugar.

Air fry for about 17 minutes, until the centre is cooked through. Test the centre is cooked by inserting a skewer – it should come out clean. Allow to cool down a little before eating.

Pear & chocolate bread & butter pudding

A crowd-pleaser of a dessert – warm and gooey bread and butter pudding with melting chocolate, sweet pear and pops of raisins. I used a large-capacity air fryer here. If you have a small one, the mix will be deeper, so you may need to extend the cooking time.

SERVES 6
READY IN 25 MINUTES

500ml (2 cups) ready-made cold custard

4 tbsp brown/demerara sugar

3 tbsp butter, melted

1 tsp vanilla extract

1 tsp ground cinnamon

4 slices of fresh bread (about 200g/7oz in total)

1 firm ripe pear, peeled, cored and chopped into cubes

100g (generous ½ cup) raisins

100g (3½oz) dairy-free (chopped) chocolate/choc chips

Whisk together the custard, sugar, butter, vanilla extract and cinnamon in a large bowl. Set aside.

Toast the bread and break into medium chunks.

Add the pear, toast chunks, raisins and chocolate/choc chips to the bowl and mix to combine.

Preheat the air fryer to 180°C (350°F) for 2 minutes.

Spoon the mixture into the base of your air fryer and air fry for 12 minutes, or until the bread pudding is browned on top and set in the middle.

Giant peanut butter cookie

If you're a peanut butter addict like me, you'll love this giant cookie! Perfect for breakfast or a delicious snack. You can add any additions you fancy: choc chips, dried fruit, nuts and seeds.

MAKES 1 LARGE COOKIE
READY IN 15 MINUTES

4 tbsp peanut butter
2 tbsp plain yogurt
3 tbsp caster sugar
60g (generous ½ cup) oats of choice/rolled oats
1 tsp baking powder
3 tbsp ground almonds (almond meal)

FOR THE TOPPING
Roasted salted peanuts

Preheat your air fryer to 180°C (350°F) for 2 minutes.

Line an 18cm (7 inch) shallow round metal baking tin with baking paper.

In a large bowl, mix everything together well to form a sticky mixture.

Put the mixture in the tin and form into a large cookie shape.

Top with roasted peanuts and air fry for 7–9 minutes, depending on how gooey you'd like the middle to be.

BREAD, CAKES, COOKIES & DESSERTS

Apple & raisin muffins

These cute and delicious muffins are easy to make and perfect for a snack, breakfast or dessert. They are sweet from the raisins, but I love them with jam and vegan cream or peanut butter.

MAKES 7–8 MUFFINS
READY IN 25 MINUTES

40g (scant ½ cup) ground almonds (almond meal)

160g (generous 1 cup) plain flour

1 tsp ground cinnamon

1 tsp baking powder

100g (scant ½ cup) caster sugar

100ml (scant ½ cup) milk

50g (scant ¼ cup) butter, melted

1 tsp vanilla extract

60g (⅓ cup) raisins/mixed dried fruit

1 eating apple, cored and grated

Preheat the air fryer to 180°C (350°F) for 2 minutes.

Firstly, mix the dry ingredients together in a bowl.

Now add the milk, melted butter, vanilla extract, raisins and grated apple. Mix well to combine. Spoon the mix into silicone muffin cases.

Add to your basket and air fry for 16–18 minutes, or until the centre is cooked through. Test the centre is cooked by inserting a skewer – it should come out clean. Allow to cool a little on a wire rack before eating.

Rich chocolate almond brownies

I'm so proud of this recipe! I wasn't convinced I could make a gooey brownie in the air fryer, but these turned out perfectly. Squidgy, super chocolatey and totally addictive. I used a vintage square baking tin in a large air fryer for this. You could absolutely use a round metal baking tin if that works in your air fryer.

MAKES 16 BROWNIES
READY IN 25 MINUTES

WET INGREDIENTS
45g (3 tbsp) butter
175ml (⅔ cup) milk
3 tbsp almond butter
100g (3½oz) dark chocolate, broken up
2 tsp vanilla extract

DRY INGREDIENTS
100g (scant ½ cup) caster sugar
50g (½ cup) ground almonds (almond meal)
50g (⅓ cup) plain flour
30g (¼ cup) cacao powder
1 tsp baking powder
100g (⅔ cup) dark choc chips, plus more to top

Preheat your air fryer to 165°C (330°F) for 2 minutes.

Line the base and sides of a medium baking tin that fits in your air fryer with baking paper.

Firstly, melt the butter on a low heat in a saucepan, then add the milk. Turn off the heat and add the almond butter and chocolate chunks.

Allow to melt slowly and stir gently to combine. Now add the vanilla extract.

Add all the dry ingredients except the choc chips to a large bowl and mix to combine. Transfer the wet mix into the dry mix and fold together to combine. Now add the choc chips.

Now spoon everything into the lined baking tin. Press into the sides. Sprinkle the additional choc chips over the top.

Air fry for approx. 20 minutes, then remove and cool in the tin for at least an hour to allow the brownies to set.

Giant cherry jam pancake

A fun to make and eat giant pancake with a delicious swirl of jam running through it. You can use any flavour of jam you fancy - I like cherry jam.

60g (scant ½ cup) plain flour
½ tsp ground cinnamon
½ tsp baking powder
130ml (½ cup) milk
1 tbsp sugar
2 tbsp jam of choice
Plain yogurt
Maple syrup

Mix all the ingredients apart from the jam, yogurt and maple syrup in a bowl to form a thick batter.

Line an 18cm (7 inch) shallow round metal baking tin with baking paper, then spoon in the batter. Smooth out to the corners.

Put little dollops of the jam on top of the batter, then swirl around.

Preheat the air fryer to 180°C (350°F) for 2 minutes.

Air fry the pancake for 5 minutes, until fluffy, then serve with yogurt and maple syrup.

Oat, banana, tahini & pecan cookies

These healthy cookies are naturally sweetened with bananas and dates. Perfect for a speedy breakfast or as a nutritious snack. Walnuts also work well here instead of pecans.

MAKES ABOUT 12 COOKIES
READY IN 20 MINUTES

2 ripe medium bananas, peeled

4 Medjool dates, pitted

3 tbsp tahini

½ tsp ground cinnamon

½ tsp mixed spice

1 tsp baking powder

140g (1½ cups) oats of choice/rolled oats

50g (½ cup) pecans, chopped up a bit

Oil spray

Handful of pecan halves

Add the bananas, dates and tahini to your food processor and blitz to a paste.

Next, add in the cinnamon, mixed spice, baking powder and oats. Blitz again so that everything is combined.

Finally, add the chopped pecans and pulse a couple of times to mix through.

Preheat your air fryer to 180°C (350°F) for 2 minutes.

Spray the basket with a little oil spray. Shape the sticky mix into small cookies and place directly onto the basket. Top each cookie with a pecan half and press down a little.

Air fry for about 7–8 minutes, flipping halfway through. Repeat with any remaining mixture. Allow to cool a little on a wire rack before eating.

Carrot cake

This cute little carrot cake is absolutely lovely. Packed with spices and mixed fruit, it can be whipped up in 20 minutes from start to finish.

SERVES 4
READY IN 20 MINUTES

DRY INGREDIENTS
20g (scant ¼ cup) ground almonds (almond meal)
80g (generous ½ cup) plain flour
½ tsp ground cardamom
½ tsp ground cinnamon
½ tsp mixed spice
½ tsp baking powder
80g (⅓ cup) caster sugar

WET INGREDIENTS
50ml (scant ¼ cup) milk
50g (scant ¼ cup) unsalted butter, melted
1 tsp vanilla extract
3 tbsp mixed dried fruit
80g (3oz) carrot, grated
Flaked almonds

Preheat your air fryer to 180°C (350°F) for 2 minutes.

Firstly, mix all the dry ingredients and a pinch of sea salt together in a bowl.

Now add the milk, melted butter, vanilla extract, mixed fruit and grated carrot. Mix well to combine.

Grease and line an 18cm (7 inch) shallow round metal baking tin with baking paper, then add the mix, spooning it into the corners and then topping with flaked almonds.

Air fry for approx. 14–16 minutes, or until the centre is cooked through. Test the centre is cooked by inserting a skewer – it should come out clean.

Allow to cool a little before eating – if you can!

index

Acknowledgements

A heartfelt shoutout to every single one of you who has been a part of this incredible journey and made this book a reality. It's you – my lovely followers of my culinary adventures – who have truly brought this book to life. Your enthusiasm, your passion for cooking up my recipes, it's all infused into these pages. This book, my friends, is dedicated to you. From the bottom of my veggie-loving heart, thank you.

Can you believe it? This cookbook is my sixth, and I'm still pinching myself. But let's pause for a moment to send out some seriously deserved gratitude!

First and foremost, a massive shoutout to my sister Ems. She's been right by my side, testing these recipes with me. And let's be real, she's never shy about giving some well-placed feedback (hint: she's got a thing for adding more cheese, and I secretly love it!).

To the phenomenal team at Ebury Press, you are my dream collaborators. Working alongside you has been an absolute joy.

My amazing agent, Malin – you're always there with unwavering support and guidance. Your belief in my culinary endeavours keeps me going, and I'm beyond grateful for that.

Last but absolutely not least, Jason and Avalon. These two brave souls fearlessly tasted their way through pretty much everything in this book. They are my taste-testing champions, love you.

So, to everyone who's brought their magic to this cookbook, thank you. Your support, love, and taste buds.

With immense gratitude and lots of love,

Niki x
www.rebelrecipes.com
www.instagram.com/rebelrecipe

4

Pop Press, an imprint of Ebury Publishing
20 Vauxhall Bridge Road
London SW1V 2SA

Pop Press is part of the Penguin Random House group
of companies whose addresses can be found at
global.penguinrandomhouse.com

Text Copyright © Niki Webster 2024
Photography © Niki Webster 2024

Illustrations: p7, 13, 14, 15, 21, 22-23, 48-49, 86-87, 89, 106-107, 158-159, 161 © GoodStudio / stock.adobe.com; p48-49 © Oleg7799 / stock.adobe.com; p86-87 © Mallinka1 / stock.adobe.com; p 7, 18, 22-23, 158-159 © K N / stock.adobe.com; p22-23, 106-107 © mart / stock.adobe.com; p 7, 18, 48-49, 51 © DiViArts / stock.adobe.com; endpapers, p. 18, 22-23, 25, 48-49, 86-87, 106-107, 158-159, 161, 191 © Lubov Chipurko / stock.adobe.com

First published by Pop Press in 2024

www.penguin.co.uk

A CIP catalogue record for this book is available from the British Library

ISBN 9781529922363

Printed and bound in Estonia by Print Best

The authorised representative in the EEA is Penguin Random House Ireland, Morrison Chambers, 32 Nassau Street, Dublin D02 YH68.

Penguin Random House is committed to a sustainable future for our business, our readers and our planet. This book is made from Forest Stewardship Council® certified paper.

With thanks to Instant Brands Limited @instantpotuk